Man-Ruling Society

Ideal Society and the First One Thousand People
by

Shahnaz Moslehi, Ph.D.

Bloomington, IN  Milton Keynes, UK

authorHOUSE

AuthorHouse™
1663 Liberty Drive, Suite 200
Bloomington, IN 47403
www.authorhouse.com
Phone: 1-800-839-8640

AuthorHouse™ UK Ltd.
500 Avebury Boulevard
Central Milton Keynes, MK9 2BE
www.authorhouse.co.uk
Phone: 08001974150

First published by AuthorHouse 4/6/2006

ISBN: 1-4259-1233-8 (sc)

Printed in the United States of America
Bloomington, Indiana

This book is printed on acid-free paper.

List of Content

About The Author

Dr. Shahnaz Moslehi was born and raised in Iran. She holds
a PhD in International Educational Planning from the University
of Southern California, and she has studied Political Education at
London University. Her masters degree is in Clinical Social Work,
and she practices psychotherapy.

Dr. Moslehi has written many books and articles. Since
her immigration to the United States, she has been involved in
both American and Iranian social political affairs by attending
related events, giving public speeches, or producing TV and radio
programs, mainly for Iranians. Her latest activity was being the
editor of a humanist magazine in Los Angeles. Having a passion
for social and political issues, she is an idealist and analytical
thinker who values humanity, liberation, and social order. She
loves nature, children, art, and music. She is residing partly in Iran,
and partly in the U.S.

Other books by this writer include:

+ An Introduction to Iranian Culture; Now in its fourth edition
in the U.S.

+ Ask Me About Me; A look at the psychology of Iranians
influenced by their history.

+ Iranian Immigrants; A research-based book written in Farsi.

+ The Search; A romantic novel filled with philosophical ideas,
written in Farsi.

+ Painful Wedding: Snapshots of the life experiences of the Iranian people under Islamic government, also in Farsi.

Introduction

In spite of so many achieved technological advancements in the past century, the persistence of problems resulting from the following facts remains a puzzle in man's social life:

Fact 1- After many centuries of so-called human progress, we are still living primitively;

a- Majority of people have to spend most of their time and energy taking care of their basic needs such as food, shelter and love, or facing the unnecessary pretensions and deceitfulness.

b- In most societies the primitive actions of aggression, violence, war, and destruction exist, and animalistic characteristics are predominant and even accepted as the rules of survival; 'the bigger and stronger one eats up the weak.'

c- The basic structures of family, education, religion, politics, and economy are enmeshed with conflicting duality or confusion over definition and purpose.

Fact 2 - The SYSTEM of economy is to be blamed for our fundamental problems, because it has been chosen as the basis for all of the set societal subsystems, and it runs through all aspects of our life today. From international policies, to our daily public affairs and our interpersonal relationships, the money, or the monetary system, is ruling.

Fact 3 - Fundamental problems require fundamental changes. The previous and ongoing efforts of patching them has not proven successful in reverse the ill condition of the system.

Fact 4 - Because the mentality of humans has been conditioned through the currently running systems, and therefore, our learned logics may limit our thinking ability, we need to detach from our learned beliefs and think beyond the existing system in order to find real solutions for the fundamental problems.

Fact 5- A powerful global core system exists and works against the people's efforts to create fundamental changes. This semi-apparent core system can now fashions as it pleases, manipulating the values, demands, thoughts, and emotions of people; and changing their ways of living as it desires. It is able to create conflict, violence, confusion, disbelief, indifference, distractions and neediness among people, to keep the people in a state of dependence on the system. It can create ignorance, selfishness and violence within a society, or facilitate full productivity and creation, all to serve the core system and to keep it running in full force. Rich or poor, entrepreneurs or working men and women, knowingly or unknowingly, they all are at its service. In fact, it is the system that, to a large extent, shapes the lives of people. However, one can argue that, in reality, it is the mental, moral, and psychological weaknesses of people that allow the system to keep on operating as it is.

We humans, like animals, plants, and other living beings, tend to establish institutions or behaviors that help us to survive and overcome our existing limitations. The institution of religion for instance, may help many of us with our "intellectual limits," and provide us an alternative to what we are not yet capable of understanding. The family institution, can help some of us to deal with our "emotional limits" and fear of total independence and abundance, it can provide us with some physical and spatial boundaries and a sense of belonging. The institution of society however, can help all of us with our "moral limits," which can be described as combination of both intellectual and emotional limits, leading to selfishness and manifested by greed for ownership and lust for control.

The emergence of current established institutions, family, economy, government, education, and religions has been to compensate for existing weaknesses, to bring harmony, and to maintain humans' mental health to secure the continued existence of the human race. However, these structures and institutions have, over time, deviated from their main purpose – the betterment of life – and have become such an independent phenomenon that shapes the lives of the people for the sake of the systems, taking precedence over the humans themselves. It seems that the purpose of human betterment of life has been forgotten, and the man has become self-estranged in the churning dynamics of these manmade systems.

It is in such vital conditions that the need for a humanist society becomes more apparent than ever. Unfortunately, due to weariness and weaknesses resulting from the effects of the current system on the minds and psyches of people, many people think that the creation of a humanist society is undoable, and they see a future of ever-increasing destruction for humanity. This pessimism is the result of the encouraged or proven belief that the essence of unleashing selfishness, the lust for control, destruction, and violence is the core of human nature, and cannot ever be eliminated from man's life. It would be difficult for most people to think differently, because people are the product of such a disempowering system.

In order to encourage others to think about and analyze the possibilities of fundamental changes in human ways of social living, this book, *Man-Ruling Society; The First One Thousand People*, attempts to think beyond the norms of existing societal structures; and by looking at the phenomena of economy, family, education, government, and spirituality, offers suggestions for a new way of social living.

A brief message from the author: Today's economic systems have kept the man a captive to his daily living expenses. It is a basic right of the modern man to be free from the primitive act of preoccupation with 'making a living.' Instead, man should be free to engage in his desired activities to actualize his interests, potentials, and aspirations. Contrary to current convictions, the improvement of the lives of all humans or the formation of a true humanist society is quite feasible. We need to check out and control both inherited and environmental factors for the appearance of subversive characteristics, such as unleashed greed, lying, and violence.

Optimism shall not be a lost cause. Any steps taken to advance our thinking, and any demand for a more humane society shall be a stepping stone toward the goal of establishing an ideal society. Please join other believers in the ideal society (Man-ruling society) and create an independent political party to provide the necessary strength and force behind the idea; or publicize it among other fellow liberated human beings.

The concept of an "ideal society" or a true humanist society is a "mission possible." Let's make it happen by taking it seriously and asking our present political representatives to consider it.

Shahnaz Moslehi; June, 1995

Section One
Why a Man-Ruling Society, and Why Now?

Chapter One:
Life in the Twenty-first Century

In the year two thousand, at the beginning of the twenty-first century, scholars from all over the world congregated in Boston, at the invitation of the American Philosophical Society, for a several-day conference to discuss the various aspects of human life and examine ways of achieving fundamental improvement in the organization of people's social life.

In the past few decades of human history, the course of societal changes, transformations in ways of living, and the nature of relationships among different societies and groups have been such that many sociologists and scholars of social and political affairs now talk about the possibility of the intensification of turmoil and violence, and about the endangerment of the continuity of human existence. These scholars warn us about the necessity and urgency of finding solutions to these problems. They remind us that the societal structures of family, religion, economy, government, and education have, essentially, not kept up with changes in human thoughts, psyches and lifestyles. In fact, many of these societal structures have become obsolete and have lost their efficiency, departing from their initial purpose.

The warning raised by these sociologists is not because of their pessimism. It is not because goodness, prosperity, and beauty have departed from this world. Fortunately for us, the pattern of life, nature, and human creativity is still alive; beauty can still be seen and created, prosperity can be brought above and experienced,

3

and love and joy can be created and felt. Even questions such as the following have not been immediate points of concern for most scholars: "Why can't everyone benefit from these endowments? Why, after at least twenty centuries of the progression of thoughts and the creation of civilizations, is the animalistic nature still predominant in humans? How come the birthplace of someone can still author her life and entitles her to, or disallows her basic human rights, welfare, happiness, or the chance to experience love and joy in life?"

Instead, recent warnings from scholars, as well as the sensitivity shown to the conditions of human community life, seem to address the ill nature of comprehensive changes that have occurred. It is a precautionary reaction to the emergence of a range of foundational problems, which can generate unplanned or uncontrolled turmoil, dissension, and destruction.

Looking at the apparent international politics and the related rules of engagement, the following fundamental problems, some of which will be explained more in chapter three, can be concluded:

+ Power Club_ Major international corporations have become too powerful. They can now shape or influence the economy, politics, laws, cultures, the content of mass media, and informal educational systems around the world, to their own will and interest.

Beneficiary owners of these corporations or the members of this well-established "power club," who are mainly unknown to the general public, have been in a position to assign governments and train political leaders around the world. Being closely and mainly enmeshed with the British Royal family, British government, and the U.S. government, these major corporations also have many loyal members in other countries, and in basically all aspects of public life, such as research, science, religion, government, and media. While supporting or creating conditions conducive to the freedom of capital accumulation in different societies, this "power club" can shape and elaborate economic systems in such a way that only a limited number of people, those who are capable and willing to play the established rules, can benefit from meaningful participation, the possibility of significant achievements, and empowering capital accumulation. What makes this condition more inhumane and dangerous is the presence of duality and double standards for enforcing rules in regards to the international politics and globalization. When discussing the economy, the utilization of resources, or enforcing international laws, globalization is viewed as a necessity and inevitable. But when discussing human rights, the principals of democracy, the separation of state and religion, and efforts for the betterment of public life, the focus becomes on the regional culture, dominant religion, and geographic political considerations.

+System Ruling_ Nowadays, with the idea of a "New World Order" coming to the surface, the outcome of man's past efforts and created complexities shall rise to a new high level; a huge international economic, political, and religious core system, which consists of series of local interrelated subsystems in different countries coming together under one umbrella; a global core system for managing the whole world. This powerful core system has also become partly self-operating, with free will, by facilitating the creation of certain subsystems that allow the core system to exist. To serve this objective, the core system benefits from the efforts of loyal members around the world, who have already become enmeshed with the administrating system and may not see any problems in following the set rules of engagement. The members of this "power club" and their associates are engaged in the constant evaluation of surrounding and occurring changes in regard to their set goals, and they often follow and promote the rules of survival or the law of nature, i.e. the bigger and stronger eats the small and weak. Therefore, these leaders and administrators may see the creation of reactionary dictatorial regimes in one region, cultural changes in one country, and the creation turmoil in another country as necessary for the management operation of the world and the livelihood of existing systems. The societal structures that were initially created to serve the needs, expectations, and conveniences of the people are now at the service of a free-will core system.

+ Money Ruling_ With the spread of this mentality, and the centralization of capital accumulation as the main purpose of life and man's daily activities, the "money," or the monetary system, has replaced the human intention in determining the shape and content of our social structures. As the desire for ownership and profit-making have been heavily encouraged, and as the "public-control factor" has been proven profitable, the man-created systems have gradually lost their initial purpose of serving people, and have shifted towards using people as a commodity for advancements in profit-making.

The ever-increasing value and role of "money" have notably been debasing, forcing people to rely only on the power of money for happiness, versus the human connection with self, others, and the universe. This growing attitude has been negatively influencing the interactions and relationships among people and societies.

+ Unnecessary Struggles_ The cognitive capacities and collective abilities of people and their nations' resources have not been employed well in finding solutions to existing problems, or to meeting the basic and fundamental needs of people. Whether in advanced industrial societies or in less-developed countries, rich or poor regardless, the people of the twenty-first century, like their ancestors, are forced, out of necessity, to spend most of their time and energy on satisfying their basic needs for food, clothing, and housing; or finding love and emotional support. In fact, in spite of progress in science and the expansion of the civilization to the twenty-first century, the ways of living for mankind have not considerably and collectively changed. For most people, the primitive struggle to satisfy basic needs has remained predominant, and majority of people have little time, energy and know-how to address their advanced needs of self-actualization, acceptance and recognition, or contentment with life.

+Dictatorships_ With the expansion of mobility and widespread immigration, the practicality of computers, and the spread of the ideas of freedom and individual independence; along with a gradual decline in people's trust in government or their willingness to follow rules, the efficacy of governments in general has been weakened or is waning out. It has been increasingly more difficult for most governments to hold on to their traditional ruling power and administrative positions. Therefore, as we have seen in the past, in many countries and recently in the United States, governments may now see the need to consolidate their positions and create a baseline for the selective use of legitimize force that serves their conveniences or needs.

+ Wearing Out_ Human mental and physical health has been a case of endangerment, if we look at the longevity of the human race and the general public around the world. Polluted air and water sources, increasing noise levels, the use of drugs and narcotics, and artificial foods poisoned by a variety of chemicals are now accepted parts of life. Also, psychological hardships have been extended due to the conflicted relationships between men and women, fast-paced and constant changes, high levels of stress, feelings of insecurity, the witnessing of widening turmoil and violence, the facing of duality and confusion, and the loss of family ties or emotional support. Collectively, these factors have driven human beings, as a race, to premature weariness of physical and mental abilities. From the loss of eyesight to sexuality and the natural ability of child-bearing, and from the loss of inner senses and wisdom to his natural ability to feel the joy of life, man has jeopardized his physical and mental health, on the altar of the continuity of the human race.

+ Elite Ruling_ In most societies today, the people, or the masses, consist of a small number of individuals with significant wealth or social power, the middle class, the working class, the indigents, the marginalized, and the convicts. Each of these groups has its own characteristics of certain ideological values and expectations for life experiences. The acquired social positions, potentials, and chances in life are essentially connected to inherited family positions or characteristics in each group that allow sufficient and timely physical, mental, social, and intellectual growth, such as access to information and individual wealth accumulation. Inter-group mobility, or moving upward, is very difficult and rarely possible for an average person.

Nowadays, heading toward the establishment of the "Ownership Societies" that President Bush has promised, having access to the right information and the appropriate use of information becomes more valuable. Soon, only those people with higher levels of intelligence, knowledge, wealth, and connections can do well or succeed. Others, or the weaker ones, as the rule of jungle permits, will have less of a chance to succeed or even survive.

Facing the above problems, man has no one to blame but himself for being in this position. There is nothing foreign and alien about this explained self-operating core system or the nature of the above problems. The subjective world of today's human being is the result of his past decisions and actions, which led to the creation of such systems. The elements or forces behind the existing complex, self-acting, and semi-disguised ill systems are nothing but manmade governments, economy, religions, media and cultures for peoples' relations.

In short, the broad foundations of coercion and oppression, the inadequacy of the existing administrative and monetary systems in solving social problems, the spread of the ideals of freedom among the people, and communication advancements, all call for new systems of economy and government. The usual systems of disguises, lies, ambiguities, and dictatorships, even if they temporarily seem workable, are not viable in the long term. Soon, those presently in power and those who have already accumulated significant wealth will have no other recourse but to help create more humanistic governments. Human history has paved the way for the flourishing of the ideas of humanism and to the creation of humanistic societies. However, governments in general cannot think and decide outside their comfort zone, their own familiar mentalities, or their own fields of interest. They are not in tune with simplicity and neutrality, or with the use of wisdom in finding new solutions. Their bureaucracy leaves little room for alternative ways of thinking. In this regard, ordinary citizens and outside observers may be more equipped to bring about the necessary changes. Thoughts and the level of support from people will set this course in motion or hasten it.

Chapter Two:
Failing Economic System

The prevalent capitalist and communist systems have proven inefficient to provide desired living conditions for their people. Also, many efforts of governments to patch up the societal systems or alter ill conditions collectively have not proven success.

Throughout history, humans have achieved significant progress in regards to scientific discoveries and man's living conditions. However, many people around the world are deprived of meeting their basic human needs and rights; and numerous social problems all over the world continue to deprive the majority of people of the full appreciation or enjoyment of the gift of life. Interesting enough, this significant and widespread deprivation is seen by some people as an unimportant or inevitable phenomenon, or it has remained unnoticed due to people's preoccupation with constant societal-induced distractions and challenges. Therefore, there has not been much cry for the fact that a new social system is urgently needed for mankind.

Today, with widespread capitalistic mentality affecting social structures, most people's daily activities have become related to gaining capital. For the majority of people, gained capital is immediately used for the provision of biological basic needs or survival. For others, the earned capital creates more "wants" and more "needs" through the encouragement of established systems, mainly for the purpose of turning the wheels of the economy.

In this process, one way or another, most of people's psychic energy is directed towards survival, and human beings are unwillingly trapped in the vicious circle of induced needs, capital accumulation, greed, struggle, and consumption.

One major problem concerning man's wellbeing is that the nature of the capitalist system is such that it focuses on efficiency or profitability only and ignores the notions of values and purpose, or the good and bad, in general. Also, as government's level of control on the economy has intensified, this system has significantly deviated from its original theoretical base, which was production in the free market, which is the decision-making of the people in determining the types and limits of production and consumption. Through a variety of administrative decisions, such as tax laws; through direct and indirect manipulation and control, such as encouraging certain values and controlling media; by determining and setting criteria in all aspects of the public domain, such as employment, communication, information, distribution, education, recreation, transportation, and welfare systems; the government can influence people's decisions choices and lifestyles and mold public opinion as it wishes. In fact, in most societies, people have turned into instruments of keeping the wheels of the economy running, according to the wishes of a few influential individuals who hold the power to elect their choice of government officials.

By looking at existing social economic systems around the world collectively and not focusing on extreme totalitarian corrupted governments or extremely poor nations, the following significant general problems can be identified:

✧ Passive involvement of most people who lack the real power to control.

✧ The brainwashing of the public by the ruling circles and the powerful.

✧ The molding of public opinion through mass media, formal, and informal education.

✧ The disappearance of the right for "selfhood" and the individual's closeness to his essence, due to the exerted social and parental molding or indoctrination.

✧ The monopolization of the mass media, which results the influence of the masses by a few.

✧ Parents and families who lack proper conditions for healthy child-rearing.

✧ Lack of accurate, sufficient, proper, and timely information at the disposal of the majority of people, combined with the significance of having information and knowledge, or the characteristics of courage, persistence, and high intelligence for seizing the power in the prevalent world.

✧ Relative deprivation of some groups, such as women, children, the elderly, and minorities, from access to social power and capital accumulation.

✧ The possibility of the spread of dictatorial methods by governments in response to the fear of social chaos and the absence of new designs for management of the public.

✧ The continuation of social disorders in the course of history and the failure of previous efforts to create humanist societies.

✧ Also, the following system problems keep pounding mankind's long-term wellbeing:

People geared towards the wheel of production

The motivation of individuals who participate in the production process is the personal gain or the benefit. The obtained benefits, however, very soon turn to consumption, which in turn immediately become a productive force. This means that people, both consumers and producers, and their productivity are part of a closed circle of production used to stimulate the economy. Also, because the goal of the economy is "efficiency" in production, people as a major resource of production will be the target of efficiency for the economy by getting involved in better, faster, and cheaper activities. In other words, focus will not be on the use of available resources to produce the needs of people. People themselves will be geared into the wheel of economy and production to stimulate more "efficiency."

Careless uses of resources

Both people and land, as major resources of production, have been used with limited care and wisdom, causing expensive or irreversible damage. Examples would be air and water pollution affecting the environment, and the cognitive emotional, sexual wearing out of mankind through drug-related problems, stress, neurosis, AIDS, Alzheimer's disease, men's sterilization, etc.

The power is a new resource for production

While people and land is being used carelessly and unwisely, leading to the loss of their future production value, access to the influencing force of "power," (political, economic, and cultural), seems to have entered into the circle of production as a major resource to shape the economy. The economic system, therefore, has become more complicated and less manageable.

Mismatch of the theoretical base with the current system

Capitalism initially was based upon the system of "pure market economy" with minimal governmental interaction, and was driven by what Adam Smith called the "invisible hand," i.e., when people are free to make economic decisions based on self-interest, they do what is best for themselves and thereby for the whole of society. However, current economic systems in capitalist societies are constantly being manipulated and controlled by various governmental policies and induced forces. This means that the base of the pure market economy is no longer available to bring about the anticipated best results for people and societies, while the initial belief and mentality related to the efficiency of the capitalism is being kept as valid.

Too much government involvement

The government has too much power and control over the economic system, as well as the people who are geared into the system. Some examples are: the ability to establish various work-related policies affecting people's time and income, the tax system, i.e., instructing and controlling the use of resources by individuals, influencing social environmental conditions related to individual choices and the use of time, such as the number and kinds of options to buy, and highway conditions; and the promotion of a certain education and certain values.

Also, the "scarcity" of resources, which is related to people's income and time as tools of decision-making, are closely geared into and at the mercy of the governmental policies. Therefore, instead of people making decisions related to their natural wants and needs and upon the availability of time, the government holds the actual power to shape and instruct the daily activities and lifestyles of people as it wishes.

Geared toward no values

The economy and decisions made within the system are not affected by values or whether the result will be good or bad for the wellbeing of people. The system only predicts the results of decisions.

Limited tools for decision-making

The system deals only with "production possibilities and opportunity costs;" and both of them are at the mercy of governmental policies:

⇨ Production possibilities are basically limited to military and non-military productions.

⇨ Opportunity costs or the priorities of spending money, which is a very complicated and value-oriented task of decision-making, often done by unqualified, biased individuals within the government who might not be sensitive to or knowledgeable about social issues and the long-term impact of their decisions on society.

No goals directly related to people

The improvement of the quality life for all and the satisfaction of people's needs and wants are not direct goals of the capitalist system of economy. Instead, efficiency, stability, and growth are the set goals and the force behind the economy.

It should be emphasized that the existence of the above problems and past failed efforts to resolve these problems should not be taken as an excuse for accepting present conditions. Obviously at this time, new thoughts and new struggles are called for, and there is a need for more flexibility and creativity in our thinking, as well as more boldness in demanding logical claims from our governments. Unfortunately, governments are mainly involved with their present or long-term interests or are concerned with their leftist or rightist inclinations. The real movements should spring out from the general public.

Chapter Three:
Upcoming Changes and Possibilities

A clear picture of the world as it will be in the coming decades may not predictable. However, many sociologists believe that existing structures for government and economy do not fit the demands of tomorrow, or even today's life. A new political system, a new economy, and a new way of social living should be developed to prevent a total and unmanageable breakdown of the existing system. They foresee the creation of new kinds of societies. Some futurists go much further and talk about a different kind of human species emerging as a result of new technology and societal changes in the coming decades.

Some of the significant changes that are already in process seem to be the following:

global government, the abuse of democracy, tension, dictatorship, elite rule, and abuse of the masses. It is worth mentioning that my focus for predictions have been more on the negative aspects of the upcoming changes, as I believe they are the overall result of both positive and negative societal changes already in process in today's world.

Global government

The formation of a world government is not far from people's expectations anymore. The direction of the development of international politics, the inter-related global economy, ongoing pressure to open borders of nations, efforts to homogenize the money market into a single currency, numerous organizations affiliated with the United Nations and World Federalist Association, and ongoing pressure to enforce international laws are all significant factors to open the door for the creation of a world government.

The concept of global government can be a positive one if all nations were seen and treated like different fingers of one hand, different parts of one body, or different children of a fair, caring parent. Although different in size or function, they all are related and nourished fully from the same blood system.

In practice, however, the global government does not promise equal treatment of the children. Some well-known social scientists, such as Noam Chomsky, talk about the ongoing deception of the masses by the powerful while describing the international politics. Also, many people, although sometimes in excess and as an excuse to release people's responsibility for the lack of progress in developing countries, present similar analogies in their formal and informal discussions about politics. In fact, today, many people are familiar with the direct and indirect influence of superpowers, such as Britain and the United States, on other countries in order to bring about changes they desire. Therefore, one can foresee that the upcoming global government may be controlled by a superpower such as the United States, which already possesses the means of wealth, arms, power, and technology to influence the world. In the fictional story of "The First One Thousand People," I have referred to this central global government as the "U.N.A.," or the "United Nations of America!"

Abuse of Democracy

Another area of concern is the ability of the powerful to control mass media. New technology has opened the doors for instant voting and the participation of more people in the process of public-related decision-making. At the same time, the monopoly of large corporations over the mass media allows the powerful to control the content and format of the available information. In addition, by misusing the science of human psychology and mind control, the owners of the media are already in the position of inducing selective values, influencing public opinion towards any desired direction, or obtaining desired instant votes from people on various issues. On the surface, therefore, this kind of voting presents the concept of free will and democratic participation of the people, but in reality, the votes are based on impulse and the raised emotions of the people, and not on their informed decisions. Obviously, the continuation of the emotional decision-making of the public can lead to dangerous outcomes or serious conflicts.

Another aspect of the abuse of democracy is when people's natural interests and values become lost in the process of social learning and assimilation, or through the ongoing influence of formal and informal public education. A clear example is when, by watching TV comedy shows with prerecorded laugh track, people get conditioned to learn when to laugh.

In a similar manner, people are given numerous ideas about the meaning of success, happiness, fairness, life purpose, etc. In fact, the media has become a significant source of power and a practical tool to control people.

Tension

Societal developments achieved and human progress have not yet been able to eliminate the need for people to compete with others for resources or the tendency to react negatively to other groups who may differ from them by sex, age, race, financial status, or social class.

The ongoing cultural emphasis on the concept of individuality, the elimination of nuclear family structure, increasing economic and social pressure on people to succeed or survive, and the emphasized benefits of profit-making and wealth accumulation, have each had a role in the continuation of this tense public attitude in the twenty-first century.

Also, new ideas and values have expanded among people, such as demanding fewer work hours and more choices with regard to work, accepting poverty as a choice, questioning life's purpose, and showing interest on Eastern philosophies or reactionary cults. Instead of conforming to the established norms, many people now select their values and choose their own lifestyles. Focusing on the concepts of beauty, love, pleasure, or inner peace; making conscious efforts to avoid competition; and staying out of mainstream systems are among the ongoing changes which will make it more difficult for the governments to hold on to their traditional position of being in control.

In addition, increasing mobility among people will create tension among immigrants and newcomers who have left behind familiar sites and values and feel the necessity to adjust to their new environments. This tension will automatically transfer to the surrounding people who themselves may be tired from the hard work and the pressure of survival, or may have learned to care less for the others, especially for those who are newcomers to their lands.

The above psychological and intellectual changes among people can bring social waves and tension, both among different groups of people, and between the people and law-enforcement authorities.

Dictatorship

In spite of the human progress in establishing more democratic ideas in its relations with others, there are some new aspects of dictatorship emerging into the concepts of "politics" and "government," partly because of the above-explained difficulty to control the public and a combination of the following factors:

⇨ Massive migration and national or international mobility among people has created a transient culture. People with less attachment to their places of origin and a limited sense of identification with their living environment may feel less obligation and responsibility for participating in public decision-making, or even following the set rules and regulations.

⇨ Public knowledge of secrecy, lies, corruptions, failures, or mistakes within the government will remain alive through the mass media and create, among people, less trust and respect for the government, law, and legal authorities.

⇨ The attraction of more people to non-conventional ideas and values, such as the creation of local governments, non-governmental societies, anarchy, tribal lifestyles, and religious-political cults will pressure governments to react and protect their own interests.

⇨ People show less tolerance for direct pressure and control.

⇨ High expectations and demands from people do not match the ability of government to take care of all of its responsibilities.

⇨ Mental saturation of people through too much information, numerous distractions and on-going financial-emotional-social pressure on them may cause people to pay less attention to their public affairs and social responsibilities.

⇨ The people's fear or anger from increasing governmental power, a.k.a. Big Brother, creates negative attitudes toward governments.

In short, the combination of upcoming societal changes, such as transient cultures, the pressure of competition for limited resources, racial and cultural tensions among people, decreasing trust and respect for governments, and the loss of traditional power and effectiveness of governments may increase the number of extreme reactionary governments. In this regard, the presence of any strong, military dictatorship or the use of force may be justified by governments in the face of massive tension or crisis as a necessity to prevent anarchy or to establish law and order as a justified dictatorship.

Elite Rule

The efficiency and practicality of personal computers, the
failure of public schools to reach people's expectations, and
high fees for private schools are gradually transferring the
public education to homes. However, the majority of families
face significant obstacles in obtaining the needed education for
their children; factors such as broken homes and dysfunctional
families, the lack of proper parental guidance, heavily encouraged
recreational values among children, the ongoing effect of social
problems such as drugs and alcohol abuse, homelessness and
poverty, selfishness and lack of responsibility, and the general
emotional burnout and exhaustion within families; all of which
have increased the number of children who suffer from limited
intellectual, psychological, financial, and social capabilities, which
are needed for healthy growth and success in life.

Although the length of formal education is not the main key
for its success, factors such as the efficient use of time, high
productivity, assertiveness, long-term planning, and access to or
use of appropriate information are the basic tools of achievement
and survival in the world today. In fact, one can exaggerate
the issue and say that in the near future, as one of the rules of
evolution, people with less knowledge and less assertiveness will
have less of a chance to survive.

Considering the significance of the access to and use of
appropriate information and appropriate decision-making, as well
as the fact that many youngsters today are getting directed to more
immediate gratification, such as sex, parties, drugs, violence,

extremist cults, and destructive identifications; it seems that only a limited number of already well-to-do and stable families will be able to provide, for their children, the education and tools that are needed to get into the circle of financial, social and political power. This will open the doors more widely to the rule of the elite.

Abuse of the masses

Even as we speak, in many countries, the focus of human rights often turns to the struggle of people for social rights and equality, while the focus on individual rights often loses color to the term selfishness. In fact, and for the most part, people's basic, inborn, and natural human rights, such as the right to an independent self, preservation of biological capabilities, mental health, inner peace, and generational survival have been forgotten.

The right to an independent self gets lost in the ongoing process of socialization and assimilation. People learn induced beliefs, values, goals, dreams, drive, and reasoning styles through the guidance of their families, schools, workplaces, and mass media; or through the established and well-advertised ideas of those who have become famous. It will be difficult for an individual to distinguish between the knowledge that is useful to understand and express his or her own wishes, interests, or capabilities; and the unfit information that is imposed and learned through a process of induced socialization.

While this widespread socialization and assimilation works against the people's rights to "independent self," it works in favor of the government. It would be much easier for any government to control the masses if people were more alike and could easily be categorized in a limited number of personality styles and interest groups.

Other existing factors on the abuse of masses are as follow:

⇨ While modern technology helps man to live longer, the pressure of competition and work exhaustion plus environmental pollution is affecting human physical and mental health in ways such as the sexuality, thinking ability, eyesight, and the inborn capability for reproduction.

⇨ Dealing with numerous and rapid changes in society requires constant adjustment and learning and may create, for some people, feelings of instability, insecurity, and lack of control. One can say that the right to inner peace, or choosing a matching or desired level to face changes, is lost in the system.

⇨ The future survival of people is bound to the level of social assertiveness and appropriate use of this information; and therefore, not only people with less social intelligence, but those with certain inborn qualities, such as a higher level of sensitivity or softness, or those with naïve, passive, and dependent personalities may have a lower chance of survival.

⇨ Science can now be misused by the powerful for inhumane purposes, such as the reproduction of people with certain desired qualities; for example, creating people with high intelligence, strong personalities to rule, the mass reproduction of unintelligent, obedient personalities to work, or creating beautiful, greedy people to deceive; in short, producing people to serve the wishes and objectives of the ruling elite who have global control in their hands.

(Ideas such as those described in this bookt have been presented and expanded in story format in an upcoming book, named *The First One Thousand People*. This book is the story of the formation of an ideal society in the year 2020).

Section Two
Stepping Stones and Philosophical Foundation
For Ideal Society

Chapter One: Definitions, Concepts and Philosophical Foundations

Chapter One:
Definitions, Concepts and
Philosophical Foundations

"If we could have started the world over again, taking into account the most advanced knowledge, including indigenous and technology available today, how would we design communities so as not to replicate the social and environmental problems of existing cities?"

Questions similar to the above, which is quoted from an article related to *The Experimental Cities, Inc.*, 1972, have been around for a while, with no success. However, we can always learn from previous efforts, profound dreams, failed plans, and their limitations such as the following:

- ✧ The Utopian city was too structured, too isolated from the existing cities, and there was too little room for people's creativity and individuality.
- ✧ The most recent similar experiments, such as the "Zegg" community, based in Germany, or the "Experimental Cities," based in the United States, are not differentiated from the existing capitalist structural concepts, and therefore, will soon be geared into the core problems of today's society.
- ✧ Revolutionary attempts, such as those happened in Russia and Iran, to bring desired social justice or create an ideal system through social changes have been too emotional and

reactionary. Those revolutions have been the outcome of built-up pressure within the system and a sudden attempt to bring widespread change.

The writer's goal for this project has been to design a small-scale, ideal model that can be into practice a cohesive "humanist society" within our present, complicated ill society. The aspiration and the effort to describe an ideal society pertain to picturing the best possible example of societal conditions that may guarantee the wellbeing of all. The hopes have been that this imaginary, yet practical, design will allow us to review all relevant aspects of social life clearly and as anew, and that it will pave the way for the next generation to make better societies. On one hand the "satisfaction of man" and the ideal life; and on the other hand, the "efficiency of society" to provide ideal conditions have both been emphasized to approach the formation of such a humanist and ideal society.

Definitions

In this effort, and for clarity of the research method, related terms have been defined for concepts, such as "ideal society" as reaching the best helping advancement and civilization for the society. In fact, the attempt to describe an ideal society model has been inclined with and extended to the writer's effort to define many related words, conditions, and concepts to fit the changing psychological and social needs of people in the twenty-first century. Some of the more related definitions are listed below, and others are presented in section four of the book, under the "What is your philosophy?" topic.

Ideal: The best possible choice, or the most objective way of thinking with good intentions and transcendental convictions.

Society: A group of people with common goals in life who live under one management and coordination system.

A Primitive Life: A life free of the following aspects: appreciation of and excitement for receiving the gift of life, being free of threats, provision for basic needs, the opportunity to fulfill potentialities such as innovations, feeling responsibility towards the environment, the development of individual capabilities, the possibility of taking care of shortcomings, the preservation of selfhood, the opportunity to satisfy curiosity and creativity, the recognition of inherent motivations, the possibility of a peaceful coexistence with other living things, and feeling free in association with others.

Advanced or Civilized Society: A society in which the basic needs of the survival of people have already been provided, and people do not have to use their energy on those primitive needs. Instead, there is much opportunity, so that the reserved energy of the individual, which is probably limited, may be used for natural creativity and production, inner curiosity, the gain of knowledge, contribution to the improvement of life for all, and the approach of ideal perfection.

A civilized society recognizes the inborn rights of individuals, as well as human nature and individuality, or the independent self. Therefore, in such a society, human inborn interests and capabilities as the source of individuality will be identified, recognized, nourished, and protected from any environmental traumas or enforced conditioning and shaping. Also, the society will control environmental factors such as wrongful parenting, harmful pressures, and the waste of individuals' potential.

Applied Humanism:: It is the application of humanist ideas into societal systems. Applied Humanism puts human nature; basic human needs; and human basic rights, such as the right to preserve self, the right to maintain self worth, and the right to be informed, ahead of other societal elements, such as the economy, politics, nationality, ethnicity, religion, and science.

Humanist Society: In a true humanist or ideal society, the running systems allow and support the elimination of the need for the rise of subversive characteristics, such as lying, insecurity, mistrust, fear, and violence. This writer believes that both inherited and environmental factors that may create those characteristics can be checked and significantly minimized through a combination of conditions listed below under the fundamentals of a humanist society

Under such condition, society will free its members from any induced pressures and threats, such as those inserted by parents and surrounding educational systems for the purpose of conformity and uniformity, or induced competition for the purpose of economic stimulation; and it will protect individuals against such factors. A Humanist Society is a society in which the individuals can possess sufficient information and knowledge regarding themselves, the environment, and the systems to make informed decisions at all times. It is a man-ruling society; a society in which the system will not automatically rule by dictating people ways of living.

Also, in such a society, while people are content with their lives, the source of their contentment is their mental health and their awareness, rather than environmental or social indoctrination. In such a society, people will enjoy the benefits provided for all.

The Fundamentals of a Humanist Society: The basic principles, such as ones listed below, that comply with the definitions offered above, regarding real progress and civilization. Those approaches necessary to organize a society that leads to provision of an ideal society are:

1. Choosing the best and highest goals, to provide good life for all human beings.

2. The coordination between set high aspirations and the ability of the people, based on their natural interests and identified collective needs, free-will production and contribution, and available resources, as well as preservation of the environment. It is a laissez-faire economy.

3. Containment of environmental threats and subversive environmental factors, such as insecurities related to threats to survivals and injustice in opportunities and advancements.

    This approach will encourage healthy interactions among people free from threats, deception, fear, and aggression. .

4. Containment of any inherent subversive human characteristics and motives, such as unleashed greed and lying, by eliminating psycho-social insecurities, and through the establishment of a proper educational system described in chapter three of the section three of this book, under the structures of ideal society, that will control inherited subversive factors and polishing human character.

5 Finally, the continuation of conscious efforts not to deviate from the path that leads to the objective of providing an ideal society with good life for all; idealism.

How to create an ideal humanist society?

When we talk about a humanist society, we mean a society where humans and their wellbeing are at the center of economic, political, and social goals and activities and decisions. In such a society, for instance, science would be used to improve the lives of humans; approaches to human growth and development would aim to recognize and realize the interests and natural talents of a person; and social life and social affairs would be conducted in such a way to maintain a person's physical, cognitive, and psychological health at the highest level. Also, existing resources would be available to all and would be preserved for future generations.

In a true humanist society, the ideal of humanism, human nature, primary needs, and basic human rights, such as the right to exist; the right to be oneself; and the right to be esteemed, involved, and informed, as being mentioned earlier, would take precedence over the usual economic, political, social, national, religious, and scientific considerations. In fact, in a humanist society, the principal goal of any economic, governmental, religious, family, and educational organization would strive to create and sustain the above-mentioned rights for all the people.

To create such an advanced and humanist society, institutions should mainly focus on the management of resources to provide the above, and to control both environmentally destructive motives, such as the tools of power and social advancement; and human destructive, motives such as unleashed greed, lies, and violence, by means of healthy management and set laws. The focus will be on raising children with polished characters who feel secure and without a need for deception or aggression, becoming the kind of people who both desire and are capable of maintaining an ideal society.

To cite an example: By just paying attention to one of the above-mentioned principles, the containment of subversive external / social factors, and with elimination of the "threat to survival," from an individual's life, affects one's state of mind, and the relationships and interactions among people will significantly be improved. Consequently, most of the lies, hypocrisies, wrong choices and decisions, insincere relations, pretensions, frustrations, mental harms, emotional complexes, and jealousy will be wiped out from people's lives.

This is a logical expectation that after thousands of years of civilization, man will be able to free himself from the bonds of basic needs, such as shelter, food, and financial security; or what

is generally called the struggle of survival. Today's man should
be in such a position to be able to use his energy mostly for
higher aspirations and goals such as love, progress and creativity.
Therefore, as a primary goal, the new social system should cover
all of man's basic needs so that he may reveal his ability, creativity,
and natural interests to satisfy his needs and curiosity, contribute
to the whole existence, and finally, turn into a more perfect entity.
In fact, if basic problems such as needs, financial worries and
the worth of money were to be resolved, changes, such as the
following, may occur within society:

* Financial worries and social considerations will not affect
the choice of marriage as it is now in most traditional
societies. There will be more love, honesty, and trust in
marital relationships, and consequently, within the child-
raising home environment.

* Parents can stay home more often with few worries, will
be kinder and more tolerant, will offer more love towards
each other and their children, and will nurture healthier and
better offspring.

* Individuals will not fall in the trap of values and lifestyles
induced by society or pressure imposed by the economic
system. They will remain as free individuals, will
experience healthy individuation, and can preserve or
enrich their selfhoods knowingly.

* Induced emphasis on materialism will be paled out, and
people will have more room for inner peace, natural

curiosity, innovation, useful science, philosophy, and humanity.

* No one has to trade off or sell his mental abilities, body, or soul. Occupations such as forced prostitution, spying, and torture will fade away.

* People will have less reasons for gathering more money or deceiving the public. Gradually, socially subversive factors will be wiped out, and the reserved energies of the individual will be spent on creativity, progress, and constructive purposes, which may lead to creation of much better societies.

Also, in creating a humanist society or maintaining a healthy society; in addition to the control of the environmental factors of need or the money factor as explained above, the containment and modification of subversive human characteristics, such as inherent tendencies for aggression and lying, would be necessary. Only those people who have polished their characters and put to rest their primitive motives can create and maintain a humanist, or truly advanced society. The implementation of this significant work and the provision of such a situation requires widespread attention to various societal structures, such as family, education, law, and economy. This high goal may be carried out through the following changes and structural phenomenon:

↳ By removing "force" and "threats of survival" from man's life through the provision of the basic needs, damaging factors, such as greed, lying, cruelty, injustice, conspiracy, the struggle to be a winner, and the domination of one group to the other will be removed.

♻ Through paying attention to children's mental condition and treating such problems as excessive dependency and lack of trust before they become established behavior patterns; by providing proper conditions for people to use their energies; and through the administration of appropriate educational, disciplinary, and therapeutic procedures devised for those individuals who fail to control their subversive and primitive tendencies, most of the undesirable features such as violent aggressiveness, cruelty, lying, jealousy, vengeance, and the desire to win at any price will be significantly reduced. At the same time, people will be exposed to proper social models and get in tune with concepts such as goodness, truthfulness, security, and mutual confidence.

The control of subversive environmental and human characteristics will allow the formation of a healthy society; a society in which the feasibility of healthy social structures have been maximized.

More so, by keeping in mind the goal of "the improvement of living for all" as a main foundation and objective, all attention will be turned to concepts such as people's, humans', and man's characteristics; nature, comfort, and happiness. Therefore, all other life concepts and societal planning, too, will be based on this consideration. Cosequently, concepts such as social and human rights, democracy, progress, civilization, economy, and politics will bear new meanings and definitions. Moreover, inventions, discoveries, and industry will find appropriate and logical direction towards the improvement of living for all; and the betterment of living conditions for the public as the prime priority on top of other priorities.

Unfortunately, at the present time, man's mental abilities and his potential for inventions, discoveries, and innovations do not have a close and meaningful relation with the welfare of the people. For example, man is able to perform the most sophisticated experiments in space or create a desired kind of life in the laboratory, but he still is not quite capable of treating the common cold once and for all, predicting earthquakes, or guaranteeing the containment of fire; and still poverty, hunger, and numerous social problems victimize a great number of people around the world.

One can imagine that the ideal, or humanist, society will be a totally different society from the one we are experiencing now. In such a society, one who has stolen an egg, for instance, will be offered an egg to eliminate the cause of his theft if that had been the reason. But the one who has intentionally told a lie will be subject to confrontation, punishment, and training. The act of lying is a deviation from selfhood and social responsibility. It is a subversive action toward both the self and society.

We need to change our views toward many of those life aspects we have wrongly conditioned to see and accept as necessity, or normal .For example, the current politico-economic system and present working arrangements are below man's dignity. Generally, it is a kind of slavery; a forced arrangement. It is possible to create a dynamic economic system based on people's innovation and natural creativity. Any external stimulating factor should emphasize an individual's natural interests and capabilities in order to preserve the dignity of humans, and at the same time, prevent the inhumane treatment of people.

In a humanist society, the possibility of people being used as the mere tools, or being "trained" for specific societal purposes through molding, indoctrination of values, brainwashing, emotional and mental influences and harms, and enforcement of rules with unnecessary objectives, . as well as the choosing a line of work by force, unfit parents, or decision-making influenced by lack of proper knowledge and misinformation should be eliminated as much as possible.

The summary of the discussed philosophical foundation

1. Economy based on free will and creativity
   Production and economic activities, plans and objectives will be based on people's personal interests and inner incentives, rather than on pressure or influence exerted by the governing system, or other environmental social factors.
2. Significance of human factor
   Child rearing and parental duties will be looked upon as a significant production activity, and only those who are fully qualified be engaged in such activities will be allowed to.

3. Seeing all human beings or the bigger picture

    People's activities and societal planning will be directed toward perfection, aimed at the improvement of life for all.

4. Significance of human character factor

    The mental and emotional injuries to children should be prevented. Damage that has been done in childhood will be diagnosed and treated before it is entrenched in the child's character and negatively affects his or her decisions and choices.

5. Environmental causal factors

    The basic needs of the individual, such as shelter, food, education, travel, healthcare, recreation, and counseling should be provided in return for one's share of participation in productivity, and without direct payment, serving to eliminate insecurity and the threat to one's survival.

6. Minimal subversive human motives

    The main purpose of education, mental health, and law should be to head off the encouraging factors of human subversive tendencies, such as violence, unleashed greed, and lying; as well as improving individuals' self sufficiency and satisfaction in life.

7. Expansion of choices

    The provision of benefiting from leisure time as one desires will be facilitated by the governing system; including the possibility of recreation, travel and learning activities, or additional production activities to earn wages.

8. Free will consumptions

   The provision of using wages and earned capital on any personal choices and wants such as owned housing, recreation, travel, additional clothes and belongings. This will be the right to make decisions, to choose, and to ensure economic dynamism at the same time.

9. Free will, creativity, and production

   People can produce and offer their production commodities to free markets in exchange for other goods, which will lead to economic dynamism, new options, and the right to choose..

10. Minimal social gap

    Lowering the gap between different social classes and eliminating the abuse of money or currency in general will eliminate the social value of money. People may not gain any additional power, prestige, or capital merely because of money.

11. Availability of guidance

    There will be the creation of twenty-four-hour counseling centers for choosing appropriate line of productive activities, skill training, leisure-time activity, or learning about child rearing, choosing a partner, maintaining health, etc.

12. Available assistance

    Twenty-four-hour centers will be created for taking care of children, patients, and the weak during emergencies, for a limited time, or permanently.

13. Flexibility

    Individuals will have the option to select the type of work and the time for doing it from among a list of productive activities needed by society, leading to economic dynamism and the right to choose.

14. People governing system

    Administrators of the society will be composed of a collection of replaceable coordinators; some are specialists and supervisors, and some are volunteers from common people who have been selected randomly through a drawing and appointed, for a limited time.

15. Idealism as the philosophical foundation

    Philosophical concepts, such as the purpose of life, the purpose of society, and the choice of social policies should be in coordination with the realization of perfectionism and the creation of a humanist society. It is believed that the human being possesses a reservoir of bright sparks of insight and an inherent tendency toward excellence. The writer, too, believes that paying attention to the inner-self and keeping the concept of "ideal" in mind as an aim and lighthouse will guide man's endeavors in the direction of true excellence and the welfare of all. In fact, if people could protect their inherited potentials from being wasted on unnecessary tasks and tension created by existing ill societies, we could have a totally different world, full of creativity and beauty. Idealism needs to become a practical concept.

This writer hopes that more people will gradually join in, and free their thoughts, and strive for idealism. More experienced thinkers, along with the new ones, may help the formation of more dynamic discussion groups, encouraging thinking, and direct people's thoughts and high aspirations towards the excellence and objectivity of the concept of humanistic or ideal society. The real problem or obstacle is that not many people can free their minds, thoughts, and logic from the limiting or restraining nature of what they have already learned and what they have been embroiled in. Also, even though many people are more or less aware of existing social realities and problems, few people believe that it is necessary and possible to produce major constructive changes; while in fact, it will be wise and necessary for common citizens like you and me, and not the established power, to combine our power of thinking with our high aspirations and build a humane society based on our own philosophical convictions. In this way, you and I, as the common citizens of this world, become the powerful and can exercise our human right to have operational power and influence on our lives. Gradually, and probably, a similar system can be arranged internationally through a global agency, branching out into various geographic regions.

Considering the above logic, the following section describes ideas as related to the significant aspects of life in an ideal society that I have put together in the last few years, hoping to develop a model which can be later modified by others for more practicality and workability. The torch lighting on this journey has been the application of humanist ideas into the societal structures of economy, government, family, and education; here called "applied humanism." The following pages reflect my efforts to describe a simple, yet very advanced way of social living for human beings of the twenty-first century; a society in which people produce and consume as they desire, yet " insecurity," "unleashed greed," and "forced competition" are not the underlying forces of production; a society in which people develop the desire and skills to remain self-sufficient, are able to choose their lifestyles intelligently, and are capable of contributing to the progress of their society and the whole world through free will; an ideal society, yet practical enough to be formed within today's imperfect and complicated society, allowing us to examine the significant aspects of man's social life today more clearly.

I believe this simple and idealistic approach can lead us to the root of the problems in our present societies, making it possible to implement the needed changes to make a better society for future generations. Naturally, talking about an ideal society may seem far from the existing reality and may sound too idealistic, but, looking at an ideal model can provide those insights that are badly needed to cure the existing social problems, readjust our goals, regain ruling power from the self-operating systems, and bring hope, comfort and happiness to more people, for the future survival of mankind.

Section Three
Proposed Societal Thesis
A Model of an Ideal,/ Man-Ruling
Society

Chapter One:
Proposed Societal Thesis to Create an Ideal Society

This model of an 'Ideal Society' presents a detailed description for the establishment of a small-scale trial community, with the participation of selected qualified individuals, to create a new societal system and new societal structures that can promise the creation of the desired, ideal society, the best possible one, and examine the validity of the presented hypothesis, below. This hypothesis suggests dramatic changes in our current economic systems and claimes to solve ongoing problems and to prevent anticipated future problems. The main obstacle is that in order to bring about any dramatic structural changes, we should first change our reasoning style and logic. Our conditioned logic may easily turn into an intellectual obstacle for finding new solutions. Therefore, we need to get away from our accustomed rationales and be able to put aside for instance, whatever we may have been conditioned to accept as a necessity for the function of the economy. One way to accomplish this objective is simplicity in logic and reasoning, by breaking the formation of each existing problem into pieces to examine the prior condition and, step-by-step, searching for the starting point of the problem. In this way, we can identify all problematic conditions before they take root within different aspects of human life and before they shape a complicated ill-societal system.

Hypothesis

Dr. Moslehi's proposed thesis for a trial society reads as follows: under specific systems of economy, education, family, and governing that have been described in this book, if the basic needs of people for their entire lives are provided, and in return they are expected to produce a certain number of time units from their choice of work, progress and economic productivity will grow quickly, and violence, lies, mistrust, and other subversive characteristics will substantially decrease.

More specifically, this thesis reads:

1. The characteristics of lies, fear, insecurity, unleashed greed, and violence are destructive to the wellbeing of mankind in any given society.
2. These characteristics are developed through both environmental factors, established societal systems, and the inherited human potential, or nature.
3. A healthy societal system can prevent the growth of destructive characteristics by the removal of the environmental causal factors and by encouraging, supporting, and following humane laws of interaction among people.
4. The creation of a humanist society is possible through the establishment of a combination of certain structures of economy, family, education, and government, similar to those proposed and defined by Dr. Moslehi in the book,

Ideal Society and The First One-Thousand People, (Man-ruling society).

Main Concepts & Doctrine

The following seem to be necessary concepts to be valued and kept by the governing system in order to promote and maintain the conditions that can lead to the creation of ideal society:

1. Recognizing the right to live; the right to maintain self worth; the right to be informed; and the right to preserve the natural self, i.e., not to be shaped or formed unknowingly or unwillingly, except to reject defined destructive thoughts and tendencies, as basic human rights, along with those other previously recognized rights of equality, freedom of speech, and choices.

2. Believing that human nature is basically good with natural desires to seek productivity, creativity, and growth; and that possible natural destructive characteristics such as lying, greed, and violence can be rejected through a healthy societal system which truly encourages raising more humane and insightful individuals, with wise and good thoughts and deeds.

3. Recognizing the notion of a "civilized society" as one with a higher ratio of humane individuals who pertain to less-destructive characteristics.

4. Believing that overly valued money and inhumane international economic systems are the main sources of many existing problems around the world.

5. Believing that the governing body of any given society, regardless of its mainstream culture, level of development, or the level of people's education, can work best if it remains fluid and changeable, holding to a group decision-making process. The common people can and should be informed and involved in decision-making. Focusing on the mentality of one group as an excuse, or any efforts to create systems of dictatorship and sole leadership are basically wrong and against humanist philosophy, and therefore, should be denounced for all nations.

6. The main goal and core objective of any society should be to take care of the basic needs of its people with food, shelter, safety, health, nourishing love, dignity, information and knowledge,, and security; while contributing to the growth and wellbeing of all human beings and not to sacrifice the wellbeing of others or the future growth of mankind to take better care of its own people.

7. Religion is a private and personal matter for people who choose to believe in it. It should not be emphasized as a separate structured entity within the societal system. Religion should especially be separated from politics and economy to prevent hidden corruption and psychological slavery among people, as well as to safeguard its nature of innocence for those who may still need to hold onto it.

8. As governing systems facilitate the circulation of knowledge and information, and as people and societies advance; notions, such as self-growth, self-directed behaviors, humanism, enlightenment, inner strength and polished souls, shall substitute the need for regulatory religions, subjective beliefs, and excessive regulatory public laws.

Desirable Conditions for Creating Ideal Society:

The following are the list of conditions to fit the proposed societal structures for the ideal society. More details for each structure of family, economy, education, and government have been presented in chapter three, as the societal structures of the ideal society model.

1. Human function and daily activities are tuned into the purpose of improving the quality of life for the self and others.
2. Societal planning and the force behind the economy are based upon the collective needs of people and their natural motives of interest, curiosity, and desire to produce.
3. There should be comprehensive public or social insurance in the areas of housing, food, education, discovery, health, recreation, and guidance.
4. Individuals share responsibility to produce for no wages, but for societal contribution or self-sufficiency, in return for lifelong comprehensive public insurance.

5. A pool of production areas, based on the objective of improving the quality of life for all, should be prepared by the governing body, for people to choose from.

6. People have choices for the type, place, and time of performing their share of contributions from the prepared pool, based on practical possibilities.

7. People can use their free time to perform other additional productive activities to earn money, working, and can use their money on any choice of consumption or saving.

8. Open markets will exist for the exchange and trade of items for those who wish to reuse and recycle, with no money involved.

9. Centers for rehabilitation of self-sufficiency will facilitate the ability of all individuals to produce and contribute.

10. Parenting is counted as a share of productivity and societal contribution for those parents and volunteers who are willing and qualify to do so.

11. Emotional and intellectual traumas in children will be prevented, identified and treated at an early age, before they can damage child cognition, emotions, and character, and before creating an unhealthy behavioral pattern in child that will negatively influence the future life choices of the individual.

12. Identification cards for the emotional, psychological, and physical health of children will monitor the achievement of the above condition.

13. There will be twenty-four hour free child care centers.

14. Self respect, self-awareness, and self-actualization will be facilitated for all individuals.

15. People can learn from each other.in creative public learning centers.

16. There will be twenty-four-hour free guidance centers.

17. A universal or international language will be taught in addition to any local choice of languages.

18. Positive human characteristics, such as honesty, courage, empathy, and the use of wisdom will be taught while discouraging subversive destructive behaviors such as lying and violence, through management, education, role-modeling and laws with respecting personal freedom and caution for possible indoctrination.

The above concepts and related functions can be implemented through the appropriate societal structures and ministries described in the following section.

Anticipated Main Obstacles to Executing and Proving the Above Hypothesis:

1- Conditioned thinking and logic of people, i.e. lack of belief or motivation to support the idea.

2- The interdependence of the economic system with other social structures, such as politics, education, family, and culture; or the complexities of present social systems in general.

The Proposed Research Method:

The author suggests getting the advice of some creative, open-minded, skilled research specialists to design appropriate methods fit to perform an experimental study of the above hypothesis in a small social laboratory with controlled conditions, such as those that have been explained in "Chapter Two: The Experimental City," and with the set objectives and conditions such as the following:

1. Aiming at the ideal or the best feasible conditions.
2. Identifying those criteria necessary for the establishment of such economic, educational, family, and governmental systems proposed in this book, which may guarantee the welfare of all.
3. Selecting one thousand qualified volunteers as inhabitants of the experimental city, in the specific age and skill categories of children, parents, specialists, counselors, managers, and reserved individuals for each category.
4. Planning for and administrating various accords needed for the provision, control, and preservation of desired and predetermined conditions within the designed research-oriented society for at least five to ten years, which is the least time needed for the execution of this experiment.
5. Aiming to observe and evaluate any practical procedure that assist and promote the creation of a dynamic society similar to the presented model.
6. Aiming to evaluate the causes of the appearance of subversive characteristics among people and within the society, or to identify the root of social problems.

7. Aiming to find an approach for improving the quality of life for all and examining the practicality and objectivity of establishing a humanist society as the best possible model.

8. Executing some similar, but larger, designs in other parts of the world, should this design and experiment prove successful, and if the hypothesis is proven.

9. Involving the general public and asking for their related advice and assistance.

Chapter Two:
The Experimental City

The basic goal for this project has been to establish a small trial community, based on a totally different social structure than is common today, and a new economic system, with the purpose of establishing the best possible quality life for all. To start the initial system, it is suggested that one thousand volunteers who meet the required criteria to be chosen as qualified volunteers who would participate in the establishment of an experimental community as children, parents, specialists, and administrators, under their choices of living arrangements, learning,and life experiences.

The effort here has been to anticipate, picture, or explain all related considerations and work necessary to implement and test successfully the proposed societal thesis in a manageable, semi-open, small community. The necessary step-by-step work has been listed or elaborated briefly in this section and below.

Initial Preparation

The preparation includes the development and establishment of different comities to do the necessary initial work such as the following:

The initial planning and administrative work; finding appropriate land, maps, buildings, materials; public announcement of the purpose and objectives of the plan; creating branches of a selection committee in various regions; the initial selection of volunteers; the final selection of volunteers and signing contracts, research and anticipation of related problems; and needed support.

Selection of the City Residents

1- Choosing one thousand people from people of different origins and types who are willing to participate in the experiment and meet set standards for one of the following categories:

   a. Five-hundred children, infant to ten years old.

   b. Two hundred parents; age sixteen to ninty; natural or volunteer parents).

   c. One hundred consultants; able to consult people on their living arrangements, job activities, child-raising, health issues, choices of recreation, etc.

   d. Fifty specialists or experts in the fields of science, space, computer, agriculture, industry, management, research, human development, etc.

   e. Fifty administrators; able to take administrative and coordinating responsibilities without personal agendas.

   f. One hundred reserve volunteers from all of the above categories.

2- Administration of a comprehensive related orientation, interviewing, training, testing, contracts, as needed and appropriate.

Living Arrangements

The suggested trial city has been set up in a way that people may have a variety of settings to choose from for their living arrangements, and most of the administrative work, coordination, and public service can be done in one central location.

- There will be ten different small communes of ten parents and fifteen children, with an average ratio of two parents for five children.

- Each commune will consist of a common living area, allowing for four different houses, which can be occupied by one, two, three, or four individuals; or by parents and their selected children. Both children and parents will choose their living arrangements and decide who to live with for certain period of time. They can change their living arrangements from time-to-time, as they wish. It is understood by all that parents may give away their job activity as parents, temporarily or permanently, to someone else chosen by the children.

- Adults and children of each commune share among themselves household chores, such as cleaning, cooking, laundry, inventory, public relations, etc.

Administrative and Economic Arrangements

- There will be a number of learning centers, theaters, restaurants, sport fields, shops, museums, libraries, and recreation centers close to people's residences; along with shaded sidewalks, with benches, all around the city, plus multiple bus stations for connection to different parts of the city or to outside the city. There is a very large hostel, or hotel, in the middle of the city as the city building for multiple purposes, such as a weekend getaway for residents, the housing of reserve staff, the housing of outside visitors, the housing of city staff, and the offices of the administrative ministries such as the following:.

Major Ministries:	Main Function:
1. Living arrangement	*Building management
	*Selection of residents
2. Reproduction	*Prenatal care
	*Natal care
	*Post-natal care
3. Health	*Physical health of residents
	*Psychological health of residents
	*Social-environmental health of residents
4. Learning	*Managing self-recognition and self sufficiency of residents
	* Inventions
	* Research
5. Production	*Planning for appropriate job activities.
	*Guidance of residents for job activities
	*Social services management (societal contributions, volunteering, wage-based activities)

6. Recreation   *Creativity and art

                       *Sports

                       *Travel

                       *Socialization

- There is a set of necessary qualifications for parenting, such as patience, the ability to nourish and guide, or the ability to seek necessary assistance. This emphasis on parenting qualifications is in line with the rights of the child to be raised free from any preventable psychological trauma.

- There will be twenty-four-hour free childcare and counseling centers available.

- In regards to the economy, the following criteria are observed: The lifelong basic needs of people will be provided, in return for specific timeshare of chosen productivity; the option of performing more than the agreed share of productivity in return for money, working; the option of spending earned money on any choice of consumption or ownership, and having no social values attached to the money, i.e. no extra power or credit, and no use of money to make more money.

- In regards to education, the following will be emphasized: natural human curiosity and interests; understanding of life, the possibility of self-actualization, the knowledge and understanding of self and others, understanding societal systems and established structure, consideration for humanity and humane interactions, and setting personal goals inclined with the wellbeing of all.

- In regards to government, the following will be observed: no secrecy policy, the free flow of information to create well-informed citizens, a fair share of residents' access to media, the freedom of choices and speech, and treating the economy, politics, and laws openly, and like any other administrative offices of the society.

- In regards to the law, the following will be observed as the main functions of the law: protecting the implementation of all identified residents' rights, facilitating the maintenance of the focus on eliminatting identified subversive characteristics within administrative systems and society as a whole; and facilitating the implementation of identified functions of all other societal institutions.

High Lights of Life Experience in the Model City

There are numbers of anticipated phenomena that may come along as a necessity or result, soon after the establishment of the suggested system in the trial city.

Computer

The computer will have a significant function in storing information and in the coordination of affairs in this trial society. The multiple functions and the significant, already established role of the computer will extend to the following,as well: population statistics; report cards on the physical, mental, and emotional health of the residents and the results of their annual checkups; coordination of affairs regarding production activities, such as one's remaining share of production activity for the year, volunteer activities, working for wages; devising a list of production services and the conditions for their implementation; educational and learning affairs; computerized counseling and guidance; responding to the questions posed by the public; the management of visits, travel or affairs regarding the residential areas; etc. The computer allows access to the information sources, creativity, and personal choices, as well as comprehensive planning, which is needed for city management.

Comprehensive Planning

The preparation of a societal system free of excessive governmental control and based on free will participation of the people calls for a high level of order and coordination. The implementation of desired activities to satisfy both the public and the coordinating team will not be realized without a precise, well-coordinated plan. In a humanist society, everyone is asked to present his or her plan for desired production services, their choice of residence, and their desired getaway or travel plan to the management group of the city, one year in advance. Residents can prepare their plan of desired lifestyles with the assistance of many provided counselors and coordinators in a format similar to the following example:

<u>(A sample case for the choice of lifestyle):</u>

Mr. X, who lives with his own two children and a volunteer mother, has a one-thousand-one hundred-hour share in production for the next year. On his birthday, he visits the management office to see if he can plan his choice of activities for the next year the way he wants, and as follows:

Five hundred hours of his production share will be completed by performing his fatherhood duties in the first three months of the year. In the second three months of the year, he will teach,part-time, in a high school to complete another two hundred hours. Then he will rest in one of the city's hotels for two months or visit another country with the provided tours. The remaining four hundred hours of his production share will be done through gardening or cooking within the last two to five months of the year. He also likes to spend some time working for wages. He will take any job that pays more, which he can perform, i.e., a difficult or specialized job that no one has taken yet, or an unpleasant one that is rewarded with higher pay. He will live through the year, except for the months spent in the hotel, with his children and the volunteer mother in one of the guest houses in the city.

Responsible Flexibility within Family

The proposed family system for the experimental ideal city calls for honest-love-based, free-will interactions among people. The aim is to eliminate problems, such as wrong choices of partnerships based on limited knowledge and wisdom, forced marriages or forced continuance of relationships, lack of responsibility, greed, excessive control, and excessive dependency. Therefore, the following will be observed throughout the overall system:

1. Facilitating for residents, the selection of a mate that will be based on sincere and clear reasons, not on emotional, social, or material needs and limitations.

2. Eliminating a need for pretentious features, such as hypocrisy and lying.

3. Providing for one's mental and personality health to nurture wisdom and a sense of responsibility in relationships and the selection of a mate.

4. Making available options for enrichment and personal growth in life and the feasibility of engaging in various desired activities to reduce the significance of finding a mate just for keeping busy and not being alone.

5. Spending enough time on the understanding of self and others for the appropriate and informed mate selection.

6. Expanding the feasibility of an easy matrimony, either temporary or permanent, and eliminating marriage obstacles, such as financial worries.

7. Putting more emphasis on child-bearing independent of the marriage itself.

8. Making a responsible and well-informed decisions regarding starting a family.

Observation of the above conditions will make the relations among men and women smoother, friendlier, and more honest;

leading to the creation of healthier families and better characters, which consequently will create a healthier society with more love and peace among the people.

Perfectionism

People with healthy and polished characters who live in a humanist society will naturally raise healthier and more sophisticated children. The kinds of individuals who are free from fears and insecurities tend to remain closer to their own nature, are content with their lives, will not violent other people's rights or disturb their fellow citizens, and are moving towards their own desired progress and perfectionism; the kind of human who, in the fullest sense, is free spirit, motivated, peaceful, creative, spiritual, insightful, natural, humane, aware and appreciating life.

We can anticipate that changes such as the following may gradually be manifested in a humanist society and towards perfectionism:

- Mental expansion and the direction of knowledge will be towards liberation, better living for all, understanding man, nature, the universe, and man's existence in its totality.
- A better use of technology will discover the potential of man's mental power and better respond to the mind's natural curiosity.
- Man's primitive destructive tendencies such as aggressiveness, greed, lying, and hypocrisy will be striven to get rid of.
- The gift of life and the worth of the fellow human beings will be valued.

Blooming creativity:

Since the energy and time of people in an ideal society will not be wasted on social environmental distractions, such as problems, conflicts, and worries like taking care of basic needs, many additional chances will be provided for people to use their imagination and creativity as they desire. In fact, the release of such a huge source of free-will creativity may result some unpredictable changes in human life and the universe. For instance, unconditional choices for choosing daily activities for people may create a barter system of economy unimaginable for us at this time. Freeing the mind from stress caused by worrying about expenses will prepare the mind to reveal its potential for creativity in all significant areas of life, including what we see now as the basis of progress, productivity and economy.

Chapter Three:
Description of Societal Structures for the Ideal Society

(The concepts have been presented briefly in previous sections)

The Family

In a true humanist, or ideal, society, marriage, or joint life of a couple, will lose its traditional complexities. All related thoughts, desires, feelings, incentives for getting married, and the purpose of it will be clear to both sides. People have the choice of simply connecting the marriage to their choice of housing partnership. Marriage will be free from the forces of given traditions, financial needs, emotional insecurities, other imposed motivations, and presently common obstacles. Also, parenting will be seen as a separate significant issue, not necessarily combined with marriage. Parenting efforts will be recognized as part of an individual's share of productivity, for both biological and volunteer parents, and children will have a say in the choice of their care arrangements. Co-dependency between parents and children will be minimal; and therefore, interactions and relationships between men and women, and between adults and children, will be based on healthy love and personal choices, facilitating healthy individuation and life-long freedom for all individuals.

In such a society, people will know in advance if the main reason and motivation for matrimony is friendship, raised interest, love, enjoying a balanced sexual relationship, childbearing, or a combination of a few. The initial duration of matrimony can be temporary or permanent, and registration of marriage would come at the time of applying for joint living or housing arrangements. Marriage cancellation or divorce happens when one or both sides asks for it.

Also, humane and legal obligations related to partnership and parenting should be observed at all time and emphasized at registration time and during the marriage. More specifically, the following philosophical beliefs and perceptions shall lead the marriage life and the institution of family in the experimental ideal city:

- ❀ Marital relations and parenting are two separate issues, and childbearing and child rearing have their own primary significance, which should not be regarded as a byproduct of matrimony.

- ❀ Parenting requires specific qualifications, such as some level of knowledge, a capacity to love, patience, willingness, and ability; versus the traditional causes of parenting, such as the norm, personal desire, necessity, or habit. Any individual, man or woman, who is between the ages of fourteen to ninety and is willing and able to provide a proper environment for child-rearing may do so. Also, interested parents should prepare themselves for the duties of child rearing and get the proper education or instructions.

❀ Mental and emotional injuries such as negative feelings toward self, others, and life; lack of confidence; low frustration levels; and hopelessness can be treated well, with the help of counselors and experts, before they take root in the personality and before they get more complicated, causing tendencies for destructive behavior or wrong choices in adult life.

❀ Human emotional dependency, rooted in child-parent, need-based relationships, will be eliminated as much as possible, allowing more self-confidence and feelings of security and independence in adulthood. In this writer's opinion, most weaknesses and emotional-mental disorders of adults have their roots in the over-dependency of a child on his or her parents. Checking such dependency at an early age will help the individual with the process of character development to become a more secure and efficient adult.

❀ The parents' role will be that of <u>guidance</u>. Among the most essential responsibilities of the parents will be the preparation of proper conditions for the child to live comfortably, safely, and securely; and to get the appropriate awareness and knowledge to become productive and self-sufficient. Moreover, the parent should be able to act as a good model of features such as justice, responsibility, self-sufficiency, production, and loving all.

<u>*Economy*</u>

The following conditions describe the kind of economic system needed to match the proposed goals of the ideal society. Establishing the below conditions allows the prevention of the rise of subversive characteristics within society, maintaining the identified characteristics of the societal structures proposed for the ideal society with such underlying results as:

- People have the control over "time" and how to use their free time to create their choice of lifestyles. Along with his or her share of job activities, one can use his free time during the year to create as desired or to do nothing; to volunteer and contribute more; to work and earn wages and consume more than his or her needs if he or she wishes to do so.

- Because there is limited time per day or year to spend, naturally, there will be a limit of how much money one can make in their free time.

- Instead of the existing profit-making motivation, the actual forces behind the society's progress and ongoing economy will be the following: the individual's natural curiosity and desire to advance; personal satisfaction and feelings of pride for contributing to the progress of the world or being effective in general; plus the desire to earn money for additional choices of consumption or donations back to the system.

The office of economy will be responsible for the adaptation of economic objectives and related planning, meeting the identified needs of people, and maintaining the foundation of a humanist society as been described and agreed upon. The proposed economy as described above rests on four basic concepts of;

* The life-long basic needs be provided in return for time share of chosen productivity,

* Option of performing more than the agreed share of productivity in return for money (working),

* Option of spending the earned money on any choice of consumption or ownership,.

* No social value is attached to money.

These basic concepts can be implemented in the economy with the following philosophical or administrative foundations:

1- The objective of welfare: By placing man and his personal needs at the center, the management of society will design a comprehensive list of the economic and productive needs of society, and of related productive activities or lines of production aimed at improving the quality of life or living conditions for all members of the society, in addition to a consideration for all human beings.

2- The contribution share: Each individual will select a specific economic-productive activity out of the prepared list and undertake to execute it. This pre-designed social share in production will be equal for all; for example, one thousand work hours per year, or twenty hours per week for ten months in the year.

3- <u>Covering all needs</u>: In response to completing one's share in production, all of the individual's basic needs will be provided for by management. People will know, from their childhood, that in return for their contributing share, their lifelong basic needs shall be provided. This arrangement alone can control most environmental factors responsible for the appearance of subversive characteristics in society.

4- <u>Maintaining individuality</u>: No hidden agenda, manipulation, brainwashing, and mass shaping will be planned, encouraged, or performed by the established system. People can recognize, maintain, and express their natural interests and talents. There will be little significant or harmful deviation from the agreed societal objectives

5- <u>Personal choices on daily activities:</u> People, based on their abilities, select their choice of productive activities from the list, along with theit choices of the time and place to perform the agreed productive participation and self-sufficiency share. For example, an individual can choose three months of teaching, two months of parenting, and five months of cooking, in different locations, for the upcoming year, all of which he or she is qualified for and can be assigned to. Today technology allows the coordination of such range of flexibility.

6- <u>Option of making money, Wage Incentive:</u> People may use their free time to engage in desired economic and productive activities and be paid for if they decide to do so.

7- <u>Personal choices for the use of money</u>: People may use the money earned by working to buy desired additional personal goods. People have the option of spending earned money on any choice of consumption or ownership.

8- <u>No social value attached to money:</u> While people can spend their money as they wish, no extra power or credit will be related to earned money, and there will be no use of money to hire others, or to making more money with earned money. The limitation of time to gain extra income, and the ineffectiveness of money in gaining more social or political power will prevent class differences, mercenaries, and inequality. But the right of ownership, saving or spending for personal consumption, will be preserved. By having no special values attached to money, external motives of profit-making and the need to have more will be controlled. Yet the personal and inner motives and individuals' choices have been maintained.

9- <u>Local exchange markets:</u> There will be a volunteer-based sector for a free-market economy within the system. People can go to an open market and trade things, such as their personal belongings or their own made products, among themselves with no money involved. This open market can be a source of recreation and fun, expansion of choices and creativity, as well as a source of healthy consumption, and will eliminate the waste of materials through reuse and recycling.

10. <u>Availability of necessary guidance</u>: There will be twenty-four hour counseling and assistance centers for obtaining information, learning new skills, self-recognition, self-sufficiency preparation, partner selection, child-raising, child care, health, etc.

Education

To comply with the demands of the proposed system, and to create healthy characters who can maintain the characteristics of the ideal society, the following considerations and arrangements should be observed regarding education:

1. Among the most important lessons and skills that the child should learn are understanding love, logic, feelings, responsibility and power, knowledge of nature and the universe, the ability to control subversive characteristics, choosing a partner, understanding of self, self-sufficiency, philosophy, religion, and management of society.

2. A child's inherent curiosity should guide the direction of education and learning.

3. Scientists and researchers should put more emphasis on "providing a better life for all," understanding the facts of nature, people participation, and creating better societies.

4. Learning can be extended to all other sections of the society. The individual will have the opportunity to access different information centers, laboratories, travel and educational tours, home-based computers, mobile libraries, lecture sessions, discussion centers for exchanging ideas,

mass media, occupation centers for exchanging skills, and expertise, in order to satisfy their natural curiosity and find answers to their questions.

5. Twenty-four-hour counseling centers will be available for decision-making, obtaining information, choosing productive or recreational activities, and any other needed guidance and assistance.

6. The direction of teaching and the facilitation of learning should be based on the level of child's social needs, actual life exposure, and necessities, such as the following model:

One to three years: Love, language, family, people, play, creativity, music, and counting.

Three to ten years: Natural interests, potential, emotions, correction of complexes, communication, environment, science, geography, computer, literature, human growth, biology and aging, and creativity and art.

Ten to seventeen years: Self-sufficiency, responsibility, psychology, choice of partners, pregnancy, child-raising, human psychological growth, emotional needs, love and sexuality, dependency, reproduction, philosophy and religion, geography and people differences, and social psychology.

___The Management of Society / The Governing System___

Type of the governing system: The coordination of society's affairs will be done by a changeable, group-based entity, which remains fluid and is open to the public for participation.

Basic Safeguards: Putting human needs ahead of other considerations, such as wealth, and the creation of a no secrecy policy, free flow of information to create well-informed citizens, fair share of access to the media, freedom of choice and speech, and treating the economy, politics, and law equally openly, like other administrative offices of the society.

Members: A combination of replaceable experts, volunteers, and randomly selected individuals from the public. This group will execute the affairs of the society for a limited time, as a part of their agreed quota for their share of contribution in production process.

Duties: Facilitating and maintaining the agreed-upon, defined elements of a humanist society, including the prevention of environmental and causal factors for subversive characteristics within the society, determining and executing agreed-upon collective goals of the public in relation with other nations, and coordinating the activities of public offices or the ministries. More specifically, administrating and performing the following tasks:

- Determination of the agreed-upon collective goals for the society.
- Coordination of activities, planning, and secondary objectives based upon the collective goals.

- Execution of appropriate and specific methods for controlling subversive factors, such as insecurities leading to unleashed greed, lying, and violence among people. This process will include the execution of such widespread overall plans, which may guarantee the following:

  a. Strengthening the healthy personality in individuals by facilitating the causal factors and freedom of choice in lifestyles and daily activities.

  b. Providing justice and equality of rights by eliminating the social value of the money in such a way that rights of ownership and the opportunity of personal choice in consumption are preserved.

  c. Providing necessary educational, therapeutic, and legal approaches for preventing any rising subversive human characteristics.

  d. Eliminating secret agendas in politics and the economy by treating politics, laws, and the economy like any other administrative organizations of society, which work for and answer to the public.

- Determination and execution of appropriate international policies that may result in the maintenance of the characteristics of the ideal society and long-term improvement of life for all.

- Establishment of needed administrative organs and ministries, such as:

  a. <u>Organization of the Habitat:</u> Manages the selection and use of residential units upon citizens' choices, such as living alone, with family or a chosen partner; in a single unit, a small apartment building, or in a hostel, for a specified time.

b. <u>Organization for Continuation of the Species</u> / <u>Office of Procreation:</u> Manages and coordinates the affairs of parents, infants, children, and youths and recognizes parenting as a job for qualified individuals. Also provides necessary professional counseling and assistance, such as proper parenting, resolving problems, educating parents, eliminating children's mental and emotional difficulties, facilitating healthy human development and constructiveness, managing the affairs of the elderly and handicapped, etc.

c. <u>Organization of Planning the Economy:</u> Adapts economic objectives, plans, and procedures to match the set goals of the ideal society and facilitates environmental conditions to meet people's needs and remain in tune with the foundations of a humanist society.

d. <u>Production Organization of the Economy:</u> Coordinates and matches society's lines of productive activities to the needs of people and the wellbeing of all, and facilitates the self-sufficiency of all citizens, covering the following areas: coordination of society's production needs with the activity-choices of people, exerting people's share of contribution in production, providing life-long basic needs of individuals, managing social services, providing equal opportunities for all in travel and recreation, helping individuals to be self-sufficient, providing coverage for shortcomings, and providing related counseling.

e. <u>Educational Organization:</u> Covers growth and counseling in the cognitional affairs of people, such as the recognition of interests, abilities, weaknesses, etc.; distributes information; facilitates organized learning, formal and informal; researches, invents and explores.

f. <u>Health Organization:</u> Provides the best possible physical and mental health, maintenance of proper environment and social life, and relevant counseling.

g. <u>Organization for Science, Thinking, and Spirituality:</u> Provides a variety of outlooks on cognition, including opportunities for learning and growth in different categories of logic and science, philosophy and spirituality, biology and life, emotions and mind, physics and energy, and society and culture.

h. <u>Organization for Politics:</u> Plans and implements the best possible approach for creating an economic system and interactions and communication within the society and with other nations of the world, all in compliance with the defined structure of politics, as it comes below.

i. <u>The Organization for Law:</u> Focuses mainly on the law, the judicial system, and on the prevention of external destructive motives, such as unjust advancements within the society, and therefore, the law will control the spread of subversive characteristics among societal institutions and the population, as is also explained below.

Politics

In an ideal society, the base of the politics will be promotion, debates and maintenance of useful ideas related to ideal society. The main purpose of the *office of politics* will be to negotiate, plan and implement the best possible economic system and best organizational approaches to form and maintain a humanist society which fits the needs and objectives of its people, while holding consideration for the whole world too.

Politics in a humanist society will be an effort to create and spread the humanist and transcendental views such as "wellbeing for all", and caring for the "essence" of humans and the value of the "nature". It will also include taking advantage of all resources based on justice, people's informed participation, wisdom and long-term based logics, and wellbeing for all.

In fact, politics will be an endeavor on the part of society's management for the protection and spread of healthy relations among the people by the supervision of social motivations relating to harmful and unjust social conducts, and paving the way for a constructive interactions, progress and civilization. (Please also refer to definitions of politics and civilization, in section four, under What Is Your Philosophy?)

The law

In a humanist society, the main emphasis of the law, the objectives of the legal system and the focus of its planning are to assist actualization of the following goals:

1. Prevention of appearance and spread of subversive environmental and human factors and imbalanced social progress in society through supervising the performance of other organizations such as the organizations for politics and economy.

2. Supporting the Production Organization for the regular and orderly implementation of the agreed upon production quota by the individuals.

3. Supporting the members of the society in provision of their basic needs and checking an orderly implementation of such a provision by the society's management.

4. Preservation and promotion of cooperation and good citizenship among people through positive models in the administration and gaining the public trust.

5. Managing setting standards and implementing necessary procedures for correcting arisen deviations from the set agreed objectives and rules, in compliance with the conditions of a humanist society. Determining and implementing appropriate approaches in confronting subversive human factors such as excessive aggressiveness, harmful lying and doing injustice (by counseling, education, treatment, forced production, denying some of the social privileges or public benefits which are not vital and essential).

Spirituality

Religious Thoughts and the Humanist Society

In a humanist society with healthy-minded secure people, religion too, will manifest itself in an ideal, or best possible, form. It means that the majority of people will leave behind their level of a primitive religion which is based on self-centered causes, such as fear of punishment or hope of a reward, and will climb to a much higher level of following a personal, informed choice of life philosophy or faith. In such a level of faith, the main urge may be for understanding the creator of the universe, which will bring about excitement, love, and admiration. It also means that man free from financial struggles, may go along with life with much more curiosity and joy, and will be interested in growth, progress and development with little fear, resentment or emotional hardship.

In a humanist society, the faithful and the faith will become one; an inner sense of belief among healthy-minded, free-spirit and free-will people. Therefore, there will be no need to determine a social position for religion or plan for its establishment, as is done for other social structures of economy, family, education, and politics.

Looking at existing religions, and in relation to the topic of this book, most religions, especially Christianity and Islam, talk about utopia, the rule of righteousness, and the establishment of absolute justice at the coming end of the world,. These faiths declare the living conditions of the final society as the ideal one. After a discussion about the features of an ideal society with some Islam experts in Iran, this writer was told that there were many similarities between this writer's proposed ideal, humanist society with what had been envisioned by different religions as utopia, or *"Madineh fazele."* Using their presented Islamic points of views, this writer identified and developed the following comparison list on possible similar topics. Also, some related explanations have been provided at the end of the comparative table below:

Ideal Society Proposal:	**Religious Approach:**
Aim of laws is to control destructive factors	The interference of religion in politics
Aim of politics is to spread the principles of a humanist society	The interference of religion in politics
Better life for all is the main goal of society	Transcendence and absolute justice.
Focus on science and philosophy together, and the laws of universe	Emphasis on secrets of creation and the collective logic of universe creation
Special emphasis on child rearing.	Child rearing as the most significant duty
Emphasis on personality development, preventing the subversive characteristics	Emphasis on human self-restraint
Idealism as the main goal, understanding humans, nature and the totality of life	A transcendence view, he/Thy instead of me.
Appreciating gift of life, enjoying life	Finding the absolute need-free and tranquil sense in praying

Also, it is said that if the principles of religion were not altered by prevalent traditions and interpretations; the similarities were probably even more. For instance, regarding what is called by some as true Islam, some Iranian Islam experts cite the following religious approaches that may create more related similarities:

Ideal Society Proposal:	**Religious Approach:**
Focus on human essence and selfhood	Significance of the parity of human essence
Parental duties as their share in production	Mothers may receive wages for parenting
Significance of self-sufficiency	Man earns only what he does
Controlling unleashed greed, eliminating social value of money	Man's righteousness overshadows material world. A need-free soul is closer to God
Ownership instinct, denial of ownership	Being free from belongings bring real freedom
Elimination of indoctrination and conditioning, the right of free thinking and creativity.	Man is created to know himself and his creator.

This writer's opinion is that, while the attraction of religion is probably an inherited instinct for man, reinforced by collective culture, the above similarities can be explained in this way: religion was originally created by the sincere and pure need of man to understand and know the surrounding world through his comforting imagination; and to overcome the fear of the unknown or existing threats. Gradually, when societies were formed, and primitive societies turned into more complex ones, people were confronted by different vital situations, which required intelligent or complicated decision-making. As man's thinking ability developed and started to find more meaning and interpretation in his social life, as new goals and needs arose, and as the need for justice or a working legal system in his social life increased; through a psychological survival defense mechanism, and to lower his level of anxiety, he was attracted to a system of thinking to substitute for what himself or the society could not provide for him. Gradually, different messengers and religions appeared and the religion was organized and turned into a significant social structure as it is today. With the passage of time, different traditions and interpretations colored these created religions with more power of secrecy, spiritual authority, as well as rigidity and lawfulness. It has been a long time now since religious belief started to enter into man's life in their different shapes, got enmeshed with and took roots in humans' actions and ways of thinking.

Today, even many of the people who, in their way of thinking, follow pure science and claim that they are not influenced by any sort of spiritualism may not quite be free of the effects of some religious convictions. Therefore, one should not be surprised to detect traces of faith-related thoughts in any logical thinking, especially when we aim to work on the level of transcendence manifestation and idealism.

In relation to the similarities mentioned between an ideal society and religious convictions, and also on the subject of the efficiency of claimed principles, the sincerity of intentions in the first place, and later, the preservation of initial principles, is very important. It has been seen frequently throughout human history that meaningful humanistic and logical ideas have been presented or proposed as principles of religion, politics, or morality; but when the public has accepted those principles at their face value, through the time, and during the implementation of the idea, the principles have been twisted around by the presenter for unjustified purposes or abuse. Therefore, and to assure responsibility in presenting any principle that carries the weight of morality or spirituality, people should be well-informed about the other related points of views. Also, the issue of people's mental health and the possibility of using fear or need to accept a concept should be discussed, and hypocrisy should be totally abolished. The well-aware public and society's managers can together prepare the right environment for the execution of desired principles. Otherwise, superstitious thoughts will spread, and some open or hidden types of human mental abuse or a mercenary system may develop. Also, it is important that religious beliefs be protected against worldly materialistic factors or political objectives and maintain their nature of incense for those who need or decide to remain frightful and religious.

Another significant point is that the efficiency of religious conviction among people is usually related to the level of individual's mental health and the health of the social system as a whole. Therefore, in any given society, and specifically in the model of ideal society, religion or spirituality, along with the systems of family, economy, education, and the governing system, should be focused on simultaneously, as one interrelated, large unit. The quality and health of each structure may affect all others.

To cite an example, in a society in which the economy is unhealthy and people are in a state of fear and need, or are angry, hopeless, upset, and feeling tired and miserable, the possibility of the appearance of a transcendent religion is quite minimal. In such a society, widespread apathy; rejection of humanism; or a primitive brands of religious mentality that is based upon the hope of rewards, fear of punishment, and blind acceptance of a fate due to being miserable, will prevail.

For a healthy society; for people who are informed and whose social relations are free from hypocrisy, insecurities, and injustice; and in a society that is dynamic and progressive, a much higher level of faith and religious conviction is called for. People should reach a point where, due to their dynamic mentality, inner peace, and free thinking, they bring their choice of wisdom and scientific logic, rules of humanity, or spirituality into their lives and resort to principles of personal faith as their guiding light in life. Contrary to common belief, getting free from economic needs, having better social and mental health, or better opportunities for learning and education may increase the chances of people's attraction to a chosen spirituality as a source for satisfying their inner needs of intellectual wondering and philosophy, curiosity, and humanism.

The state of fullness in mind is an inner feeling, and the faithful may learn it, but in practice, a constant involvement with the making of a living, the threat to one's survival, and concern about the future and injustice in society will create hopelessness and will reduce the shine of inherent goodness in people. While in a reverse situation, when the rate of social subversive characteristics are reduced, optimism takes root in people' hearts, and the individual's inherited goodness will find a chance to manifest itself, and more humane people with good characters will appear. Good human beings are in a better position to demand and build a better society.

Section Four
Ending Notes

Chapter One:
The Summary

The Summary

It was my inner motive and belief in the feasibility of creating a humanistic society that led me to an open invitation in Los Angeles in 1993 (Appendix # 2). My initial objective was to encourage intellectual discussion and find answers to questions such as the following:

1. Is cultural, mental, and social confusion, which is apparent in many countries, a normal and natural path towards man and society's improvement? Is this path unavoidable, and should we simply accept or welcome it? Or should we improve and change the path, and if so, is there a possibility for doing that?

2. Why are some people happier in their lives, and what is the main cause for this? Is the happiness a natural or mental capability? Do random chances and simple happenings or fate, the predetermined shape of events, have a significant role or function in our way of living? Or is it just our mental capability, learning, and opportunities provided by society that are responsible for the extent of happiness in one's life? Why are only a small percentage of people who have had enough opportunities content with their lives and enjoying inner tranquility?

3. Are the inherited differences of individuals, in categories such as intelligence, beauty, creativity, and persistence, the very beginning of discrimination?

4. To what extent are wise thinking and logic teachable?

5. Why did Marx fail to form his ideal society, and why have similar experiments failed?

6. Are inner motives enough to stimulate people to work, create, and produce? Or is the actual need or application of some outside force required?

7. If the need of "making a living" or payment of expenses is removed, will greed, lying, insecurity, and wrongdoing among people be reduced?

8. Who are the society's actual parents? Aspiring people like you and me?

9. What is the most significant problem or shortcoming of man today? Is it a social, philosophical, or inherited one?

10. Is the increase of the power of religion in recent years responsible for the rejection of or weakness of philosophy?

11. Is it the individual who is ultimately responsible in his life, or should parents or government to be held responsible?

12. How do the present societies seem and to what direction are they moving? Are they moving toward the destruction of older cultures; widening the gap between different classes, people, and governments; the spread of greed for the accumulation of money as life's main objective; or faltering philosophy?).

. . . .

In response to my curiosity and the above questions, I went back in time and envisioned the primitive life of a small group, focusing on the beginning of man's social living. I imagined how people's social life took shape, how a society was formed, and how it gradually turned unhealthy and contaminated; looking for environmental or social subversive factors.

In this search, the one shining subject seemed to be need and its related insecurities. Then I turned my attention to people's inherent characteristics or the philosophical reasons for the appearance of social problems. In this, what occupied my mind the most was man's inflated greed. It seemed that, while the desire to own may be in one's nature and an inherited instinct, greed for possessing more is a learned phenomenon that thrives in the family and is also encouraged heavily in the present societies, resulting in subversive personal and social characteristics among people and numerous widespread problems within societies.

Therefore, to create better societies and contain such deep-rooted needs and desires, the provision of ideal conditions deems necessary; conditions to provide for the complete health of the individual, family and the social systems.

It is in this process that the characteristics of an ideal, or truly humanistic, society forms in my mind, and the concept of "ideal" loses its imaginary and inaccessible reputation and turns into an objective matter to be pursued. The aim becomes focusing on the concept of "ideal" as the best possible condition and as a requirement for approaching the betterment of life for all, or creating much better societies.

To define and picture an ideal society, the main features of a true, humanistic society, with its focus on human needs and human control, with one thousand imaginary inhabitants in different categories of ages, sexes, and specialties; was suggested to be formed inside of such a well-defined experimental city explained in this book and described below:

- A city in which the individual is not shaped by family or society. His first human right,that is individuality or selfhood, is observed, and his capabilities and interests are identified and nurtured.

- A city in which mental and emotional damage to children is prevented. Their personalities are recognized, and their shortcomings are identified and corrected, early in childhood.

- A city in which the people have no motive for lies, hypocrisies, violence or fear-based reactions.

- A city in which, when one wins, it does not mean that someone else has lost, but all are winners.

- A city in which activities' motives of feelings of need and force and the primitive goal of providing a means of living has been removed and replaced by people's inherent aspirations to grow, produce, create, and reach perfection.

- A city in which mere politico-economic consideration has lost its influential ground.

- A city in which man is not a captive of social systems.

- A city in which the economy and production are based upon the desired activities of the people and their informed decisions.

. . . .

In designing such an experimental city, one thousand individuals will be selected as the first inhabitants of the ideal society, according to some clear criteria such as age, sex, and other characteristics described in the book. Then, under special conditions, they will start a new social life as an experiment. In this book, a full chapter has been devoted to a detailed description of the fundamental structures of the experimental society and a full chapter to the implementation of the project.

Some of author's underlying ideas and beliefs, which led to the writhing of this book and elaboration of her concepts for the establishment of an ideal society, are as follows:

* While mankind's efforts and hard work seem to be necessary for a dynamic economy and the ultimate goals of better living and reaching desired growth, the existing focus on the mere objective of profit-making and the belief that no better economic system can be developed is questionable.

* Capitalist and socialist systems are both old and decayed, because at best, they are based on man's struggle for survival. Today's man does not need such a struggle and has already passed that phase.

* Third-world countries should ignore industrialization and enter the era of computers at once.

* It is no longer possible to stop unemployment. Man's creativity and energy should be devoted to something else. Present working habits are captive and sort of mercenary.

* The new economy should be around technology, communications, getting rid of ownerships, moving toward globalization, and adjusting to liberal values.

* Politicians and government agencies are so involved in the process of problem-solving, self-protection, decayed traditions of the right or left, and playing the game of politics, that they are not in a good position to present long-range and progressive plans. Proper and useful steps should be taken by people themselves.

* Precision, punctuality, and planned production should be expected of machines, and not of humans, and not by force. Those features can kill man's creativity and confidence if they are fear-based.

* In modern life, communication is instant and direct. The computer can directly connect us to the source. The middlemen, such as representatives, teachers, secretaries, or shopkeepers, are not needed systematically anymore, but by choice only.

* The relationship between politicians and mass media in today's world has achieved a socially dangerous status. Together, they can divert our attention at their will. Common people should have more of a share of access to the media.

* It is also clear that the fear of controlling information belongs in the past. Today, it is almost impossible for any power to control the spread of information for a long time. The flow of information sooner or later will spread all over.

* When we look at different countries around the world, we realize that something is wrong with our definition of education, and that the heavily publicized modern educational system has failed to create better characters and healthier societies.

* Universities have lost their proper path by focusing on the training of mere specialists. Specialization alone is not enough. It will be more efficient to nurture proper character and humanist values, and to promote the mental and social health of the people.

* Most educational systems of the world today still stress on planned uniformity for individuals by educating them in such a way to enter the work market, form a family, and facilitate governmental control. It is not humane to ignore one's nature and kill one's individuality through a planned shaping and continuous indoctrination. We should allow true independent thinking and decision-making from the people.

* Some elements of ancient educational systems, such as having a personal guide, or tutor, in life; taking part in small classes; and learning the skills from skilled people of the neighborhood, still can be effective and useful.

* All schools should be closed to remind us that the whole world is a school by itself.

* The languages that should be learned are as follows: An international language to communicate verbally and in writing; a language of love and emotions; a language of logic; a nonverbal language of metaphors and movements; sign language; a language of numbers; a language of animals and other living beings; and a language of nature.

* The principles of education should be teaching love, logic, responsibility, human interactions, selection of friends and spouses, understanding emotions, group dynamics and societies, the preparation of experts in a self-leadership society, space, science, philosophy and theology, motivation versus greed, controlling harmful emotions, and self-sufficiency.

* The extent of one's tendency to get married, desire for possession, and one's tendency to be attracted to a faith are related both to one's social and family upbringing, and to one's inherent characteristics, such as dependency, courage, curiosity, greed, selfishness, self-confidence, objectivity, or subjectivity.

* It is required that parents be qualified for parenthood with knowledge, the ability to show love, patience, and willingness.

* The intense dependency of the child to parents following pre-birth dependency in the womb may be one source of a child's weakness and insecurities in adulthood. It would

be wise to let the child associate with different people to reduce his or her dependency on the parent.

* It is necessary to diagnose and treat a child's. This approach will prevent emotional and behavioral problems which are due to internalized wrong beliefs of early ages, and keep individuals from making the wrong decisions in adult life. Mental and emotional shortcomings should be corrected before they leave a permanent mark on the child's personality

* One may ask whether there is a relationship between one's responsibilities to the self, society, or humanity as a whole; and the extent of one's contentment and happiness in life. If one is dissatisfied with his life, can we expect him to put the society above himself and feel responsible, too? Does responsibility not mean a struggle to preserve something which you appreciate having received, like the gift of life, or the society you live in?

* New social laws are needed for a humanist society. Whose crime is heavier: one who has stolen an egg, or one who is lying? He who has stolen an egg should be given an egg; he who has told a lie should be punished.

* Does today's struggle for survival imply that the uninformed should be perished early?

* Is it a good idea to issue an emotional, mental, and intelligent identification card for children?

* How can we break the silence of the silent majority and cause them to move?

* In the eyes of society, the ones known to the public pay a high price. Who are those who may volunteer or accidentally join the process and are willing to pay such a price?

* It is necessary that a larger group of people choose to enter the forum of social activities as their profession or main interest. They may, for instance, join the green group to protect the environment or a true human-rights group, not metaphorical or hypocritical ones, who are involved in the protection of humanism and people's rights. They may form a group to reduce the rapid progress of technology or to direct its progress to a desired path to serve the welfare of all. Or they may join the proponents of an ideal society. If necessary, they may establish a party, representing a formal group, and promote the principles of their ideal community.

Chapter Two:
What Is Your Philosophy?

The human psyche is mainly formed by one's conception of its relationship to the environment, other people, and life experiences. From the four pillars of one's personality (The definition of personality is presented in this section and on the following pages), only one pillar can be consider innate, and the rest are formed in relation with the environment or the society. Therefore, one's "social psyche," or what he feels at any moment about himself within society, becomes the center and core of his personality, guiding his daily choices and decisions, and therefore, influencing immediate and far social surroundings, society, and the world, as well as how his own life's quality may turn to be.

Today, considering the complexity of modern societies, paying attention to the social psyche of a person is both a humanistic point of view and a necessity. The most emphasis should be put upon the formation of one's identity and character, and on the interdependence of man and societal systems and how they appear, develop, and change each other. Attention should be paid to questions, such as the following:

In what ways may affection and love for all thrive in humans be secure? How does identity, interdependence, and need get formed and manifest itself? How do people learn logic or choose means of problem-solving as an individual, or collectively as a nation? How do emotions, such as hope, happiness, fear, indifference, excitement, rage, doubt, hate, frustration, and apathy, get formed;

and what is the border between the positive and negative feelings or a productive and destructive attitude? And at what point does the individual lose his power of decision-making to the system?

Because of remarkable environmental and social changes in the past few decades, the human mind, probably being a social creature, has also changed. Therefore, at the onset of the twenty-first century, a new look at the psychology of modern man and new definitions for related concepts are in order. We cannot be satisfied anymore by the offered definitions of the past century, or be ready to accept only those definitions offered by known sociologists and a limited number of writers. To come up with true, collective, and meaningful definitions, we need to distance ourselves from conventional ways of research and reasoning. All people should be encouraged to identify and express their views, senses, sources of connection, and their personal beliefs or philosophies in regard to the significant aspects of social life and human psychology. This approach may seem impossible, because it contradicts what we have been conditioned to accept as necessary criteria, or practicality, and what we have already learned about the meanings of psychology, sociology, education, specialists, qualifications, communication, teaching, or methods of research. Therefore, this suggestion may look impractical or unreasonable, but the significant point is that the principle of the idea; considering the value of all individuals and one's power of thinking, one's freedom to define his own psyche, and the effort for the feasibility of collecting people's points of views for understanding them are all in line with the features of a humanist society. Therefore, finding an approach for its implication can be done, too. For example; there can be discussion sessions in each city, daily, weekly, or monthly, among small groups, and a definition of concepts may be sought. There can be contests regarding the topic, and new opinions and definitions can be collected; and after reviewing and considering all collected definitions and comments, and only then, some new definitions can be presented by the specialists. Naturally no one's definition may be quite free from past learning, and there will be some similarities or repetition of what has already been said by others. That should not undermine the whole concept of gathering public opinion for the purpose of finding more relevant meanings.

For the encouragement of this practice, the writer defines in here, her own understanding of, or her personal definitions for, the following topics:

What Is Your Philosophy?
(Concepts in one statement)
Philosophy:

Philosophy is broadly conspicuous thinking or the ability to become a philosopher, which depends on the possession of various mental capabilities, such as the vision or wisdom' broad and deep thinking; insightfulness; the power to scrutinize, analyze, and elaborate; the power of connecting facts together; varied experiences in life; and extensive knowledge. Aside from extensive knowledge, other capabilities of these kinds that are necessary for an individual to become a promoted philosopher may occasionally exist among uneducated people, too. For example, the following simple parable heard by this writer from a countryman, in regard to birds eating and destroying the products of his walnut tree, may reveal the point:

While beating up the branches of walnut trees to gather walnuts, two countrymen were speaking together. One of them complained that the crows caused damages to many walnuts by pecking at them and eating them away. The other countryman disagreed and said, "in fact, the Crow is a fair bird; she picks only her fair share of the things."

If we pay good attention to this simple statement, we will find multiple philosophical concepts in it, such as:

1. Birds and other animals, like humans, have characteristics, such as fairness.
2. Fairness is a good characteristic to have.
3. Animals, like humans, have some given rights.
4. Every entity or creature has some predetermined rights in nature.
5. Although a man plants a tree and waters it to grow, that tree does not belong to him. It belongs to nature; to allow other creatures to use their share of rights and benefits from it.

Is it necessary to wait for years for these philosophical sparks lit by a countryman occur to a scientist or known writer, then get introduced to us as a theory or judgment to be incorporated?

It can be asserted that there is a latent philosophy in the minds of most people, and it would be a humane effort, which would grant benefits to the community, too, if we can awaken and recognize these forgotten philosophers.

Freedom:

Freedom is an innate feeling or belief in the ability to perform or receive a well-deserved right in a specific situation, along with a clear and complete vision of its righteousness. In other words, the lack of freedom can be defined as the combination of the following situations:

1- A true demand, not a manipulated one, of a personal or social nature;

2- A belief that the same demand would not hurt others;

3- An informed belief in the existence of some identified or unknown unjustified obstacles to obtain that righteous demand;

4- The evolution of negative emotions, anger, furiousness, despair, hopelessness, anxiety, etc., due to the existence of deterring factors;

5- And the inability to remove deterring factors.

Emotions:

Emotions are a psychological response, resulting from a recorded cognition or belief; or the evolution of feelings, such as disgust, joy, sadness, anxiety, excitement, and apathy; leading to the appearance of some concrete behaviors or responses, including the behavior of controlling responses. Emotions are any mental belief that creates special feelings leading to a related choice of response or behavior by the person. Examples are:

1- The belief that "I am not as good as others" may create negative feelings toward oneself and anger toward others; leading to the choice of isolation in behavior.

2- The belief in the need for hiding self-recognized weaknesses may create anxiety and defensiveness, leading to efforts to deploy aggressive behavior, or to manifest itself as a wide range of self-reliant activities.

Greed:

Greed may be a congenital derivative, but is mainly an acquired and internalized belief of the need or desire for boundless or unnecessary ownership.

Ideal:

Ideal means one's mental ultimate destination, or to meditate and mark the way to go forward as correlated to one's perception and will. To employ all the existing possibilities which create uplift for a chosen mental target. An ideal means the best that is possible and the possibility means recognition, comprehension, requisition and employing all assets.

Contrary to what the public thinks or what has been previously publicized, the word "ideal" may carry an objective sense, and its pragmatic performance could be more clarified provided it be addressed further by scholars.

Personality:

It can be said that there are four pillars of personality, and that they are shaped in the following manner:

First pillar: The combination of hereditary characteristics; that is to say, our natural and inborn structure, or the kind of mental-intellectual characteristics, or capabilities and tendencies with which we enter this world.

It appears that the following principal trends are the constructive hands of our primary personality pillar:

1. The traits of "giving versus taking" tendencies: the "giving" tendency may co-exist with characteristics, such as self-indulgence, kindness, tenderness, and leniency; and the "taking" tendency may co-exist with self-centeredness, selfishness, high-expectations, dificulty-to-please, and perseverance.

2. The traits of obstinacy and resistance versus the traits of lesser resistance and inborn susceptibility, or vulnerability, in regards to life challenges.

3. The innate ability for mental growth, covering the limits of intelligence, ingenuity, learning, analysis, and reasoning abilities; as well as accelerated emotional growth.

4. The innate ability to grow emotionally in proportion to age, covering one's potential for responsibility adoption, sensitivity to others' situations, patience and tolerance, control of feelings, and the extent of expectation from others.

5. The extent of optimism versus pessimism, or the potential to have a positive or negative view of life, which may be embedded into the inborn category of "giving and taking" tendencies. It appears that those who have "giving" tendencies may enjoy more positive points of views in life.

Accordingly, the type and extent of the combined characteristics inherited by the individual will influence his mental ability, his attitude in life, his daily choices and decisions; and consequently, will influence his kind of future or life experience. For example, an individual whose predominant traits are those such as sensitivity; pessimism; vulnerability; a limited capacity to grow emotionally; along with a "taking" tendency, which creates high expectations, and therefore, more possibilities of disappointments, would be more liable to be exposed to depression and dissolution.

Some published medical literature, such as *Kaplan and Sadock's Synopsis of Psychiatry; Seventh Edition*, published in 1994, has extended the previously known extent of hereditary influence on the formation of human personality. For example, consider whether the following cases are congenital or hereditary characteristics: Degree of physical activity; rhythm of sleep and digestion; temperament quality, meaning good or bad temper; level and severity of response to environmental stimulants; level of tolerance for stimulus; level of concentration; depth of feelings; potential for avoidance or challenge; and finally, limit and speed of adjustment to environment.More have been followed since then.

Second pillar: The configuration of original primary beliefs, such as, "I am good, others are good, life is good, I can trust, I can survive safely," are required for the psychological health and balance of an individual. It is said, and it appears that these beliefs appear at the early ages of three through seven years old. What is more significant in psychology is the continuation and extension of these established beliefs of childhood to the mentality of adult years. That is to say, when a child has been convinced by reasons of his experience and his childhood interactions that, for example, he is not good or he must not trust; then he most likely will not be truly convinced that he is good or can trust others, despite his developed intellectual ability to observe and comprehend the reverse-proving information as an adult. Consequently, he may experience some reinforcing bitter experiences and emotional problems in his adult life.

Third pillar: The period of puberty or the depth of a puberty crisis can be considered another pillar in the development of an individual's personality. It is in this period that one's recognized "identity," separate significantly from their parents, and gets formed. This includes how and how much can one recognize and appreciate his own identity as an individual, or "personal identity"; as a male or female, or "sexual identity"; as a member of the society, or "social identity"; and his existence as a human being in relation to the whole universe, or "philosophical identity."

Fourth pillar: It consists of the varied experiences of childhood and adulthood life, including the result and impacts of the ongoing experiences of establishing relationships, pursuing personal goals and dreams, and how those already-established beliefs are adjusted, amended, or reinforced through daily life experiences.

Maturity:

It means a mature and fitted thinking, feeling and behavior reflected by an individual in relation to his age, social expectations, and situational realities. It consists of the two traits of mental maturity, as related to logic, thinking, and social apprehension, and emotional maturity, as relating to one's feelings, emotions, and how an individual relates to others.

It seems that puberty is a mental capability, and some may naturally have it more than others. At the same time, it is necessary to note that the variety of life experiences, proper and timely training, healthy social relationships, hardships, and the need to assume responsibilities can force a person to undergo mental and emotional maturation.

A low level of intellectual and emotional maturity may manifest through the following behaviors or characteristics: problem with establishing relationships, low self-reliance, manipulative behavior and the telling of lies; the use of subtlety and tricks to abuse one's positions; low tolerance for the acceptance criticism; a loss of control over one's behavior and emotional responses; a feeling of being oppressed and subject to wrongdoing; an inability to anticipate one's behavioral consequences in a timely;

the avoidance of responsibility or accountability for one's conduct, that is to say, laying the blames on others; and a difficulty in exercising discipline, order, and planning if suggested by others.

Also, while the two co-exist together, mental or cognitional maturity may have a positive effect in reaching emotional maturity.

Love:

Love, in general, is an internal voice of the individual that makes a promise to satiate some of his or her known or unknown biological and psychological needs; including the need to connect, enjoy, own, give, be useful, produce, reproduce, or satisfy some kind of emotional emptiness and insecurity. Love among people is an internal voice which is based on an instant conclusion or the ongoing analysis of one's computerized mind; an unconscious analysis of all data related to the individual's needs and how another person may satisfy those needs. The involved needs can be emotional and sexual, or related to finances and identity. They can also be extended to some abnormal psychological need, such as self-punishment. How much love one may feel for the other person depends largely on the anticipated result of his or her mental analysis of the limits and the possibilities of the respondent in regards to the satisfaction of the identified needs.

Faith:

The presentation of faith has been different in all corners of the world, and among different groups of people in different historical periods of time. Religion has been the most prevalent form of faith until now. If it was possible to recognize the religious beliefs and practices of common people in different places and times, we may be able to introduce the following divisions in regards the question, "What is the faith or religion?":

1- An curious internal force to know the unknown and satisfy one's intellectual wondering.

2- A need to feel safe and sound, a mental or ceremonial approach to lose the fear of the unknown.

3- A learned and internalized belief about a set of possibilities based on reward and punishment and losing the ongoing fear of sin.

4- A pretext of an individual to control and abuse others. A choice of strategy to satiate one's greed with wealth and power, or to satiate one's own identity needs.

5- A systematic cat's paw of government used to control masses of people and communities.

6- A belief to guide others that may result in an effort to do so, and may possibly create a religion. This effort of a person may be based on a genuine belief, a feeling of a spiritual responsibility, a lie, a hidden plan and pretense, or just a response to an existing psychological disorder of the person. The limits of success in this effort depends on the truthfulness and integrity of an individual's mission, as well as his intellectual capability, charisma, and supporting resources; the recipients' mental maturity and emotional needs; and societal situations at the time.

Ownership:

Ownership is a psycho-cognitive process: "Me, my needs, response to my needs." It starts with a demand for a thing to satisfy some identified need or want of a person, then leads to his or her effort to obtain and maintain that satisfying thing.

It so appears that the sense of ownership may initially be an instinctive cognitive process, beginning with identifying the need: "My being, my hands, my mouth, my hunger"; A response to the need: "Mother's breast and the satisfying milk"; and the effort to obtain the satisfying thing: "Crying, catching the breast and sucking."

If a sense of ownership is primarily instinctive and kept initially for survival, the child will learn soon about the meaning and significance of it through environment. When the caregivers provide personal objects, such as a pair of shoes, clothing, and toys; then repeatedly emphasize that they belong to the child, they will create a new image and weight regarding the concept of possession and ownership. When the child grows older, he learns again, from his parents and from other people, the importance of ownership of things such as a house, furniture, money, and wealth in general; and hence, assigns more value to ownership and gets introduced to greed.

It appears that in the adult age, when an individual decides to take a spouse or mate, the initial child-mother relationship may evolve again, turning into new ownership feelings and new dependencies to satisfy marriage-related needs. This process may manifest as feelings of insecurity or envy towards the spouse.

The author presumes that the ownership of things, known as assets, is unnecessary and even irrational for modern men and women. If major needs, such as houses, furniture, vehicles, and communication instruments were considered public utilities, a wide range of savings would be accomplished to the benefit of all communities, and a great deal of possibilities would emerge for people to move forward.

People Well-being:

It means living with a good and satisfying quality conditions, which facilitate and provide desirable living standards in all aspects of life, as described below:

- The continuing and timely supply of all substances and food that are needed for our bodily systems, such as protein, minerals, and vitamins.
- The possibility of healthy and continuing satisfaction of one's sex, as derived from the early period of puberty.
- Extended comfort, satisfaction, and security, regarding housing accommodations.
- Extended comfort, quality, choices and variation for clothing.
- The continuity of the feeling of having love and being loved by others.
- The possibility of maintaining one's dignity and self-worth in relation to all others.
- The possibility of following through with one's personal curiosity and goals.

- The possibility of maintaining selfhood and the emergence of personal interests, strengths, and potential.
- The possibility of correcting weaknesses.
- The possibility of reconciling and adjusting oneself, or relating to the social environments of family, society, and other communities.
- The knowledge and awareness of oneself, others, the environment, the world, and the universe, as well as the best-used cognitional, emotional, and behavioral ways of connecting to them.

Considering the above criteria for people's well-being, one can decide which communities have, in fact, turned their attention to take the necessary measures to provide a true well-being for their citizens, which is the definition of an advanced society.

Civilization:

Civilization is a cultural dynamism, or an advancing change of mental activity, spirit, way of living, and constructiveness; as well as better control over factors deterring constructivism, such as poverty, inequity of harshness, mental and bodily endangerments, environmental destruction, etc. Civilization means living better than the past, in regards to thinking and relating, creativity, comprehension, physical and mental health, character, and societal systems, that covering more number of people.

In fact, civilization is when the majority of the people of a given society can accomplish the following; and any community that would be able to provide more of these for a greater number of people can be called a civilized society:

1. Getting rid of man's primitive subversive characteristics, such as feelings of insecurity, excessive selfishness and greed, lies, aggression, the loss of the selfhood, and being incompatible with other co-existents.

2. Getting away from the primitive ways of living that are vulnerability to natural disasters, from having to consume most of one's energy on survival-based activities and satisfy basic needs, and from being under the control of unwanted systems.

3. Using more mental capability and creativity for the well-being of more people and the building of better societies.

Mental Health/Psychosocial Health:

A true healthy-minded person is the one who, with complete awareness and wisdom, and without harming others, would like and be able to make all possible efforts to employ some of the existing possibilities for enjoying his life, improving life for others, or advancing the universe and life in general.

Such an individual needs to be in tune with the psychosocial perspective and have the following personal and social characteristics, most of which have already been listed by Abraham Mazlow, the eminent psychologist, who has presented one of the best common definitions about a sound personality in his time:

1. **Good Character:** A lack of threats, or threats which are successfully defeated; particularly threats against primary

beliefs regarding the self and the world in general, such as "I am good," "I can trust," "I am loved," and "life is good." Also, the possibility of developing healthy character with feelings of responsibility; the desire, motivation, and effort to improve one's and others' standards of living; and the elimination of negative and degrading emotions such as envy, malevolence, shame, despair, and selfishness.

2. **Satisfied Needs:** The ability to satisfy all basic needs regarding the necessities of living, safety, love, feelings of belongingness, identity, self-worth, and dignity; the loss of all fear-based insecurities and the need for control, greed, lies, aggression, and war.

3. **Actualization:** Independent thinking and desire, motivation and possibilities; the use of effort for advancing self, communities, and the world; and the use of all inborn potentials and existing possibilities.

4. **Social Wisdom:** Necessary social awareness, strength and power, such as knowing and understanding societal structures, recognizing and being aware of the environment, soundly judging with regard for the whole, understanding and recognizing social entitlements, creating a true civilization, or bringing wisdom and long-lasting peace into the societal-structures and the existing world.

Considering the above characteristics, it can be claimed that, in existing modern societies, only a limited number of people are actually enjoying complete mental health with a useful psychosocial perspective.

Chapter Three:
Personal Notes on the Preface

Having always been fascinated by thought and analysis, one beautiful autumn afternoon, waiting behind the steering wheel of my car in a traffic jam on the Los Angeles freeway, bubbles of thoughts flooded my mind and broke one after another:

"Life is so good and precious... Not so many people around the world feel this way... Realistically, can all people spend every day of their life just the way they want?" The lightness of this thought brought a smile to my face. "How about me, what is it that I want the most?" This serious question brought a shade of thoughtfulness to my face. My lips pursed, and my eyes narrowed as I searched my mind for the answer. "Do I know my real interests and dreams, free from the influence of my surroundings?... Have my beloved parents, teachers, and elders not shaped my beliefs?... Do I have an independent self within me, or am I just a random product of societal rules and norms?... Who am I?... What kind of emotional and intellectual trauma did I go through while growing up? .I asked myself, feeling sorry for my beloved, forgotten, real self... What will happen in the future? Will I be happy and safe?.. Am I guaranteed life-long security for life's basic necessities? `Probably yes, as citizens in the twenty-first century, we can have every thing that we want. ",I said to myself. "Yes, of course, and all of us have the right to have at least the basics`.

A loud honk from the car behind me broke my chain of thought and brought me back to reality. Seeing the angry look on the face of a well-dressed woman who was pointing her middle finger at me made me feel embarrassed for being so dreamy and wanting to change the world from behind the wheel of my car.

Pressing the accelerator and turning the radio on, this time I thought about the realities in today's society. All learned knowledge, my feelings and desire, latest heard news and facts and possibilities mixed together in my mind over the shadowing voice of a news reporter in the radio:

** The spread of radicalism, hardened religious or nationalistic ideas, suicide attacks and mass killings, extreme reactionary actions by governments, revolving family structure, and raised tolerance of people for aggression in the world.

** Confusion about the changing concepts of identity, morals, and values.

** Increasing bias, hate, and separation among people of different groups and the trouble-inducing culture of profit making, spreading all around the world and in all aspects of human life.

** Attempts to create and gradually implement, throughout the world, a new way of living, a new, yet not-well-known system for social, political, economical affairs of mankind.

** Attempts to create a global, central government with elite rule, dictatorship and control, and possible abuse of the mass.

** The creation of reactionary options, such as free-love communities, religious cults, and racially separated communities; or the creation of new experimental cities with a new face, yet still based on capitalist principles, bringing false hope to people who seek drastically needed social changes.

For a moment I noticed a glance of sharp light from the sun and seeing the colorful clouds in the sky and the beautiful open fields around the freeway awakened in me a sense of appreciation for beauty of the nature and joy of life. It reminded me of the simplicity of life pleasures and the existence of man's natural freedom. My skin absorbed the warmth and colors of the sunset. A zest for life ran through my body and awakened in me a desire to live fully and search for the "real me," an attempt to set my selfhood free again.

All of a sudden, everything in our world; we the people, our guarded or competitive interactions, our politicians and the systems which we have created seemed unwise and childish. I thought to myself again; "We may think we are very advanced and complicated, but for the most part, we are acting like immature children fighting with each other for different reasons, making loud noises about existing political problems, and not paying attention to the fact that the very cause is our own way of thinking and reasoning. Our logic has created the way this world is. How childish we have been… How the world would turn around if we could see things differently, think simpler and be wiser!... But how should we change, and where should we start from?"

A big bubble of thought jumped out to entertain me!: "Sometimes the least suitable or thinkable option may bring the best results. The possibility of forming a successful experimental city in one of the radical developing countries in the Middle East, such as Iran, may bring needed attention to the actual definition of advancement, civilization, human rights, and democracy!."

Traffic was getting lighter now, and I was able to move forward faster on the freeway. At the same time, my feelings and my thoughts were getting lighter and lighter, too, until from the essence of eternity and insights planted in us, some bubbles of creative thought found their way into my mind, bringing ideas and hope for a possible mission: a vision to create an ideal society.

When I finally arrived home that evening, I had a mental picture of an "ideal society" and the upcoming fruits of such a society for mankind. I knew then that I would be writing a book about the "ideal society" very soon.

Interestingly enough, while the creative part of the job, which was coming up with related concepts and conditions for creating an ideal society, as well as the description of how to implement those concepts, were done shortly afterwards, within a few months, it took me more than ten years to publish the book, mainly due to the problems of same societal barriers raised in the book.

I am thankful, however, for having the chance to do what I really enjoyed doing, and .I hope that readers too, enjoy reading my writing.

Section Five
Appendix

Appendix 1:
Who Are We?

Supporters of Applied Humanism

Who are we? We are you and I, and any other world citizen who has been attracted to this topic. We are anyone who likes to support, promote, practice, or discuss applied humanism and request the application of humane ideas into the societal structures of family, education, economy, and into established political systems around the world.

Applied humanism means putting human nature, human basic needs, and human basic rights, such as the right to preserve the self, the right to maintain self-worth, and the right to be informed, ahead of other societal elements, such as the economy and science.

In fact, in a humanist society, the core goal of the economy, governing system, family, and education would be to establish and maintain the above-mentioned rights, along with all other previously recognized human rights for all human beings. Applied humanism means bringing humanity into the societal systems of government, economy, education, and family; and therefore, into the core systems of character shaping, while recognizing religion as an individual personal choice outside of societal structure.

This author believes that overly valued monetary and inhumane international economic systems are the main source of existing problems around the world. To make a better society and to achieve real advancement, we, as the entity of people and government, combined, instead of allowing economic considerations to shape our lives, must focus on the needs of human beings. Equally important is creating better and healthier characters who can and care to create a better world for all.

Similar to the nature that holds within and circulates both birth and death, the human mind has roots in two opposing energy sources of positive and negative thought, capable of creating growth or destruction.

* In fact, the collective thought of human beings in each period of time determines the pattern and level of growth and destruction in the world.

* Has your voice or opinion been heard yet? Have your thoughts been counted among the collective thought of your time? Have you had the opportunity to feel connected to the life on earth, beyond yours?

Author's underlying beliefs for establishing or supporting goals:

* Political affairs and quality of life in developed nations are influenced by those of less developed countries, and visa-versa.

* Ultimate wisdom rests on goodness and fairness.

* Nowadays, political, cultural, and economic independence is not realistically possible for all nations; taking the following steps as long-term and short-term goals are necessary and urgent to de-escalate widespread violence around the world:

Suggestions of Goals for the Supporters of Applied Humanism:

Long-Term Goals:

1- Creation of a recognized political party in the U.S., or within the United Nations, to promote the establishment of Humanistic Governments around the world.

2- Establishment of a Humanistic Global Economy, starting with serious efforts to provide a minimum life quality for every individual around the globe.

3- Empowering an international criminal court system with the notion of no nation being above the law.

4- Establishment of a true democratic world government, with equal presentation of all nations, regardless of their economic power, or, the elimination of national borders and citizenship among all participating nations.

Short-Term Supporting Goals:

1- Dispatch of a humanist representative to the Unites States Congress.

2- Establishment of a democratic republic, in Iran, with separation of religion and state, to stop the spread of racial and radical religious views around the world.

3- Having a representative in the future government of Iran promote the formation of the Humanist Republic of Iran.

4- Introducing to the public the content of the author's proposed societal thesis, presented in this book, for the purpose of:

1- Testing the level of practicality of presented ideas;

2- Finding solutions for existing obstacles;

3- Identifying and presenting other similar possibilities and options.

In short, the goal is to create strength around implementation of the indicated objective: To support, promote, and discuss "Applied Humanism" and the application of humanism into the structures of family, education, economy, media, and government.

* * *

Appendix 2:
Writer's Public Calls

WARNING: President Bush's plan for an "ownership society" leads to elite rule and a more aggressive society, leaving more people behind through the race. The spin of two opposite sets of words and actions will create a confused culture and make it difficult for people to separate truth and righteousness from lies, wrongdoing, and destruction.

A citizen, Shahnaz Moslehi, publicly complains against President Bush for causing unnecessary psychological and financial instability and hardships, and against the deprivation of the liveliness and rights of thousands of people around the world to preserve the independent self, based on the following:

1- Undermining the principal values of democracy and honesty by justifying recent national and international undemocratic actions as a necessity, and a model for the use of violent force, leading to the spread of "legitimate" dictatorships around the world.

2- Choosing the goals of profit-making and business interests, and not public needs, as the main inspiration for policy making and allowing the system of economy to rule man's life instead of people. Consequently, creating profitable corruption and undesirable businesses that work against public interests, and negatively affecting the environment and the character shaping, lifestyle, and general wellbeing of many people around the world.

3- Choosing the wellbeing and prosperity of American people over other nations, while practicing a leadership role over international affairs and inducing selective U.S.-serving economic, political, and cultural changes in other countries.

4- Creating unrest and tension around the world through the support or enforcement of shortsighted and unfair international political-economic policies that keep alive the destructive circle of force, struggle, lies, mistrust, hatred, terrorism, and war.

5- Empowering radical religious groups by inducing feelings of fear, anger, insecurity, and hopelessness among people, and creating additional need and desire for blind faith.

6- Undermining the decency and independence of human thinking by strengthening and establishing a powerful monetary materialist cultural system that requires certain characteristics and conditions to compete and win. Through daily advertisement and cultural teaching, this system is extremely overvalued and blindly desired by most people who unknowingly and systematically have been conditioned to consume, desire, and need more.

7- Detouring from policies that can facilitate good character, wisdom, peacefulness, enlightenment, and habitual choices of good deeds.

8- Limiting support for the use of pure imagination and wisdom to create better societies and a new economy by mainly supporting those ideas and conditions that are made to fit into the current system of economic and corporate mentality, and matching only the existing, familiar ways of learned thinking and logic.

9- Cooperating with Britain, who, historically plays shadow politics by weakening people's ability to understand and participate in political process and supporting and manipulating the spread of extreme faith in developing countries to keep them behind.

10- Supporting a weak United Nations not capable of fulfilling its duties and responsibilities of protecting equally the economic rights of all member nations.

01-17-05 Shahnaz Moslehi, Ph.D.

www.appliedhumanism.com

*** A Public Call for Bringing Life Into the Life Situations (06-10-04)*

It is true that, in spite of the apparent madness, there are so many good things happening around the world, and life is so good and full of promise for many of us who can feel the joy of life within, or have achieved many desirable life situations. It is also true that our manmade societal systems are turning man's destiny toward division, mass brainwashing, justified control, lawful dictatorship, emotional instability and powerlessness.

What kind of future you would envision and choose for yourself:

1. Being a part of small, elite group with power, the winners, and letting the majority of people, the losers, struggle in poverty, illiteracy, submissiveness, violence and war?

2. Or Living even better than now while all others enjoy the good life and witness gradual elimination of violence and poverty around the world?

If you choose the winner/loser option, number one, you can be sure that your mind has been strongly poisoned by the existing systems of family, education, media, economy, and government; and your current thinking is weak in reception of your own inner wisdom. This is not an insult; it is a fact.

If you think that the win-win society, number two, is not a realistic one, and that the current system of governing world affairs is the best one possible, you can be sure that you have not yet used most of your inherited creativity and insights.

Whoever you are, it would help both you and the world to put your trained mind and learned intellect to rest, periodically and temporarily, and allow your true creativity and inner wisdom to rise up even higher, creating new ideas for making the option of a win-win society a reality.

Nowadays, the "overly valued monetary system," combined with "unfair systems of international politics" continues to influence the quality of life around the world and guide people's ways of thinking, lifestyles, and interactions. The results have been reactionary inhumane acts of violence for some, and emotional instability and ignorance for others. We people, as a whole, and each of us individually, need to strengthen our position by polishing our character with wisdom and courage and take practical steps to polish and correct our societal systems. This can be done by taking two easy, yet significant, steps:

A. Become an honored member of Good Character Creation Club (GCCC), which is based on what you already know about the universal, old-fashioned concept of "good man and good deeds."

B. Become a supporter of applied humanism, raising the possibility of people truly using their ruling power to put the notion of human wellbeing ahead of monetary systems and profit-making. This change in focus at least provides a minimal level of quality for all to start with, and is urgent and vital to preventing additional violence and division among people around the world. Better life for all is a possible mission. Please review the presented information on the GCC Club and the Proposed Societal Thesis on this Web Page: www.appliedhumanism.com.

* * *

Appendix 3:
Good Character Creation Club

Introducing the idea of GCC Club (June 2004- www. appliedhumanism.com)

The GCC Club membership (Good Character Creation Club, suggested by this writer and an imaginary one at this time, will be established in near future) is about appreciating one's personal decision and efforts to present and maintain good character. Good is what your inner wisdom knows as good. Wisdom and goodness work well for true living. This writer believes that true living is; when you are aware of a joyful life within you, when you have a good and wise purpose in life, when you can choose, when you wonder and go after natural curiosity, when you create, and when you change.

These states of true living are closely connected to good character, as it eliminates the reasons and need for pretending, lies, fear, and insecurity. The following are good questions to be asked:

Have you been truly living today?
Have you been a member of GCC Club today?
Have you ever enrolled your children in this club?
Has your inner wisdom been awakened lately?

The decision for membership in GCC Club is a joyful game and an honorable play to be a part of. It is free, informal, playful, and all in your hands too!

When you become a loyal member of GCC Club you will live even better than you do now. You will belong to this club when you truly believe in good character. Those of us who honor all the rules listed below shall automatically earn the membership of the club for the period of honored time. Frequent relapses from membership may happen and are anticipated.

Rules of G.C.C. membership:

1. Believe and be open to the idea that people are basically good in nature. What may seem bad today is a bodily action, hollow of inner wisdom; or a wrong behavior learned and encouraged through an ill system of character shaping.
2. Start from knowing yourself, and practice "true living" as defined above.
3. Develop a general sense of acceptance for self, others and up-coming events.
4. Do not criticize or judge bitterly yourself, others, and life situations.
5. Listen well; listen through your heart.
6. Be fair, and be sure that you have done the right thing.
7. Do not lie, have courage and respect yourself and others.
8. Do not fear.
9. Forgive and let go of negative emotions.
10. Initiate love and smile.
11. Be kind and give love for the sake of love only.
12. Show sympathy and show respect.

13. Search to see the unique beauty of all other beings.

14. Keep secrets. .

15. Do not lose your inner source of hope and joy, see life as an adventurous trip.

16. Create, express, and share humane ideas and spread the goodness around you.

GCC Club Membership Benefits:

1. Establishing sharpened sense of real self and coherent life principals.

2. Sense of pride in choosing or belonging to a prestigious club which is based on reaching out for higher standards for human deeds and a better quality of life.

3. Setting a clear and good model for your children, to guide them in life, and to support, comfort, mentor, and remind them as needed.

4. The option of receiving support from other members of the club, ones you get to know among your associates and friends or through local gatherings or internet connections, during expected frequent times of relapse from your membership.

5. Opportunity to stretch your power of practicing self-discipline on a chosen focus, daily and hourly, to maintain club membership.

6. Creating a network of new friends and associates with similar life principals for yourself, your children, in your neighborhood, and around the world.

7. Creating your own local group to discuss related topics.

8. Any other possible benefits that you can add, such as having fun with keeping track of your own membership status.

9. In the shallowness and harshness of the systems surrounding us, being light and following the rules of this club to maintain membership reflects quality character in the public eye if it matters to you.

10. Belonging to the GCC Club, even for only one day or one month, regardless of being recognized or acknowledged by others, is an exclusive, honorable membership to be proud of.

* * *

Appendix 4:
The Story

(Ready for a movie-making and to be published as a book in near future)

It is the year 2020, and an urgent meeting is being held at the White House in Washington, D.C. The participants are the President of the U.N.A. (United Nations of America, a central international government of Planet Earth), three other government officials, and fifteen invited guests; all respected sociologists, humanists, thinkers, and artists with various origins of nationality.

Ten years prior to the date, two female presidents, one from the United States of America and one from Britain, collaborated and used their negotiation skills in the United Nations to call for a central international government to govern all nations of Planet Earth under one rule.

At the same time, various small, experimental cities had been established around the world to study human behavior and create a more manageable system of economy and social rule, befitting people of the new world who were increasingly more mobile and expectant.

The first selected president of the central government was of Chinese origin. He implemented the aggressive use of power and forced to establish what he called "cooperation and order." Soon, it was obvious that his strategy was not working well. Unrest increased, and many nations requested to drop the agreement and withdraw from central government. The experimental cities were falling apart, and the most successful one of all, which had been established in a radical Middle East country, was sabotaged to fail by some secret political agencies. People were angry, and the level of frustration and hostility was rising. Rumors were spreading about the central government giving priority to the space-related advancement and the creation of new human species and a plan for abundance of the planet earth. There was little hope of managing the system of the newly established global government.

The second global president was a black male of U.S. origin. The hope was that his election could decrease the rising tension. This strategy appeared to be working well, but it resulted in more uprisings and social-political-racial economic instability. Various pressure groups, religious, alternative humanistic, and racist, were forming and creating more diversity, chaos, and anarchy.

International consultants were called in to form a committee to develop a radical, yet practical, plan to create some immediate hope for improvement of interrelations, as well as the quality of life for people of different nations. After several meetings, the committee members were called in to put together their suggestions and start implementing their plan as the top priority of the central government.

This "action committee" consisted of seven social scientists and philosophers with different origins of nationality: a young, French / Iranian woman who introduced the main creative idea related to the new societal structure; an older man, a philosopher from Venezuela who works collaboratively with his wife, who is a well-known Russian human biologist with controversial ideas about scientific biological experiments;, a male writer and artist from Mexico; an Iranian man who is a creative educator; two people from the United States, a woman who is a specialist in space communication who takes over the administration and coordination of the committee, and a man from the international security agency; and finally, a young woman of Chinese origin who is a specialist in communication and public relations.

The initial plan was presented, by the Iranian woman / French philosopher, to the action committee for debate, modification, and development of details.

The basic plan was to establish a small trial community, based on a totally different social structure and a new economic system. It was decided that one thousand volunteers who met the required criteria be chosen to start an initial system with the purpose of improving life for all. This system was to be used later for larger trial communities, and would eventually to be introduced to various nations around the world.

The book, *The First One Thousand People,* soon to be published, will be about the formation of that initial ideal society. The story would be in novel format, focusing on some interesting, ongoing events behind the formation of community. The book covers the details of the plan, the logic, the criticism related to many new and creative ideas, as well as anticipated problems and challenges as they occur. It also contains intellectual debates and disagreements among different scientists. The story has interesting main characters, and focuses on their emotional strains, uncontrolled romances, and surprising deceptions. The book creatively demonstrates the strengths and limitations of mankind for adaptation, and the possible challenges ahead for the creation of an ideal society.

Read this book and receive a shower of interesting ideas. After reading this book, you may decide, after all, that you would like to be a volunteer, participating in creating a trial city based on the ideal model presented in this book.

The End

www.ingramcontent.com/pod-product-compliance
Lightning Source LLC
Chambersburg PA
CBHW061258280526
45784CB00002B/802